THE HOLLOWED HEART

Blessings for the journey,
Deb

THE HOLLOWED HEART

———— ❧ ————

Inspiration for Women
Awakening from Grief and Loss

Louise Dunn & Deb Buehler

Peace to your heart, always,
Louise

Mill City Press

Mill City Press, Inc.
212 3rd Avenue North, Suite 290
Minneapolis, MN 55401
612.455.2294
www.millcitypublishing.com

ISBN: 978-1-936400-71-3

LCCN: 2010940714

Printed in the United States of America

DEDICATION

This book is dedicated to the countless women who have gone before us in the human family, women who experienced and survived profound losses. We each walk on the sacred ground of their combined wisdom, strength, and courage.

It is further dedicated to the amazing women who bravely share their stories of grief and healing in these pages. For your voices we are immensely grateful.

Finally, it is dedicated to you, our sister traveler on earth. We honor that your story of grief and loss is unique. We hope that you will give your process the loving attention it so deserves.

CONTENTS

Companion Me

Companion me in my days of pain;
be near me though I may push you from my side.
Care about me
though I may seem uncaring toward you.
Stay with me through this dark night of my soul,
and do not hold me to a timetable
of your expectations.

Believe in me and in my ability to heal
until I can remember
how to believe in myself.

Love me – not from a "safe" and detached distance,
but from the holy nearness of Spirit
within both of us.

Speak gently of me
when talking to others about my trials.
Speak up for me
if anyone should deny my holiness.

In your thoughts and in your prayers,
hold me in the light of sanity and radiant health
until the darkness finally lifts
and I can once more see
the face of God within my own smile.

Companion me, my friend,
until we can commune again as in the days gone by.
Then I shall say your name in gratefulness
and at Heaven's gate announce you as
the angel of my soul.

– Louise Dunn

Let us remember that the greatest gift we give to anyone in pain is just to be there, a loving presence without judgment, reservation, or expectation. In the safety of this love our dear ones can find the hope and strength to heal.

CHAPTER ONE

Reframing The Experience

"Women, I believe, search for fellow beings who have faced similar struggles, conveyed them in ways a reader can transform into her own life...Women catch courage from the women whose lives are writings they read, and women call the bearer of that courage friend."

– Carolyn Heilbrun,
The Last Gift of Time: Life Beyond Sixty

Joyce's Story

My family consists of a husband, a daughter, and a son. Matt, my son, was killed in a car accident when he was seventeen. My husband and I were in Florida for a short visit with his family. I had a sense of urgency to call my son back home in Indiana. When I called, Matt answered and said "I just walked in the door, Mom." We talked for a while and he told me that he was so glad I was his Mom. This seemed like an unusual thing for a teenager to say. I asked him why he would say that. He explained that I was so flexible. We said "I love you" and "good-bye." That conversation was to be our last. He *died that very night.*

What I needed most in those days of initial shock of Matt's death was for people to listen to me or accept my silence without trying to fix my grief. I had some people in my life who were able to be with me in my sadness. My sister, my best friend, and my daughter were good examples. I realize that the desire to fix someone's sorrow and help out is strong, but really, it's just not possible in a lot of situations. The person must be given time and space to get through the loss. In my opinion, the only really appropriate thing to say is, "I'm sorry." Comments like, "Just be grateful for the time you had with him," "He's in a better place now," or "Why don't you try golf, country line dancing, etc." just don't help!

I still miss my only son deeply, but I don't cry so much after fifteen years. What helped me deal with this loss was the care and support of my minister, my sister, a best friend, and the regular meetings with others who had experienced this kind of grief at The Compassionate Friends group.

Note from Louise

As a minister and life coach, I have looked into the face of grief countless times over the years. The story of Joyce and her son which you just read was placed here because Matt's funeral was the first one I was called to do as a newly ordained pastor. I was totally unprepared to help this family through a most devastating kind of loss, that of a child. Yet trusting something deeper inside us, the grace of God and the humanity which linked our hearts, we somehow managed to find inner strength to walk through that shocking and profoundly sad experience together.

Herein lies the clue to surviving grief and loss — *the companionship of others*. We cannot do life alone; we are hardwired for relationships and meaningful exchanges. Our joys and our sorrows need to be shared so that joy is expanded and sorrow is eventually absorbed and healed.

So many people have no frame of reference for handling the inevitable losses of life. Our society as a whole seems often clueless about how to help us through a time of grieving. It is as if we are supposed to hurry up and be "normal" again so other people can feel better in our presence. But losses change us, sometimes forever, and there is no way to "hurry" through bereavement. It is a process that takes time and attention. Each individual grieves differently, and everyone deserves to have their process honored.

It is our deepest wish that as you bring your own grief and loss to the pages of this book, you will feel companioned and understood, that you will find relief for yet unexpressed emotions, and many ideas for honoring yourself through the difficult passages of your life.

Grief and Bereavement

Because of the confusing or ambivalent messages we internalize around the handling of loss, we may not be aware of the difference between the experiences of grief and bereavement.

> **Grief** is the normal immediate reaction to a death or loss. That reaction can involve physical, mental, and emotional responses.

> **Bereavement** is the extended period of mourning following a loss in which we experience our grief and process all of our responses to it. It is only through allowing the bereavement process that we find healing.

The human experience is so deep and rich and wonderful. At the same time it is fraught with tremendous turmoil and great pain. We simply cannot avoid the grief and the losses that are part of living. We can only hope to find the courage, strength, resilience, and grace from those who have gone before us to walk through the difficult passages of life.

In this book you will find the stories of other

women who have traveled their own path of grief. Their words give us a window into the unexpected depths of bereavement and all of its complicated, soul-wrenching facets. Their voices also provide encouragement as they bravely claim their own healing.

In our society, we are still often very sheltered from the temporal, ever-shifting nature of our life on Earth. So when we are faced with a great trauma or a significant loss, we may stumble in the darkness of ignorance with little or no knowledge of how to proceed.

When we are going through a difficult passage in life, it can be very easy to get caught up completely in it and to wallow in our pain. There is grief in any big change, and the process of grief for many people is sticky; they may want to push it under the rug and ignore it, self-medicate so it won't feel so bad, or just fail to attend to it. Most of us are raised without a frame of reference and without role models for grieving or for handling traumatic change.

Anne Lamott, in her book *Traveling Mercies*, suggests:

> *All those years I fell for the great palace lie that grief should be gotten over as quickly as possible and as privately. But what I've discovered since is that the life long fear of grief keeps us in a barren, isolated place and that only grieving can heal*

grief; the passage of time will lessen the acuteness,
but time alone, without the direct experience of
grief, will not heal it.

What To Expect

When we go through the personal experience of a sudden or traumatic loss, we can be thrown into a condition some authors call "grief brain." This little phrase is an apt description for the many reactions that are almost universally associated with grief. We will talk about these throughout this book, but we feel it is important to briefly describe a few of them right here so that you, the bereaved reader, can see that these are normal responses.

Here are some reactions to loss that have been reported to us:

"I could make all the really big decisions needed immediately after my husband's sudden death, like how we would handle the funeral arrangements, but the little daily decisions like what to wear and what to eat were almost impossible for months."

"I swing back and forth between total numbness and unbearable sadness, and I don't even know which is worse."

"Sometimes I think I'm going crazy or senile; I can't remember where I put things just moments before, and I'm snapping at anyone who tries to help me."

"There are times when I feel like I'm not in my body any more, just hovering outside of it somewhere, watching myself go through the motions of life like a robot."

*"I can't seem to find the motivation for **anything** – it's like I just don't care anymore, even though I know I 'should'."*

Simply stated, the above statements reflect these characteristics of grief brain:

- Numbness
- Confusion
- Mental fog
- Difficulty focusing
- Difficulty making decisions

While it is absolutely true that no two people experience grief exactly the same, it is also true that we can find similarities and themes in what we all go through in our times of grief and loss. It will be important for you to talk about what you are going through, to share with those you trust the sense of shock and the feelings of being drained, stunned, and overwhelmed. Everything that you experience is normal to you, but you might not be able to honor your own process without the tender sounding board provided by others.

Tell Your Story

When we are stuck, we keep doing the same familiar things, always expecting a different outcome. Until we shift the light on our experience and begin to see it from a little distance, we are caught in its vortex.

Telling our story is one way to get more light into the pain of our experience. It helps us glean new meanings from the trauma or loss we have just gone through. Re-framing begins in hearing ourselves put words to our deepest emotions, thoughts, and questions. Something physical, at the cellular level, begins to shift in the re-telling of the experience, giving it room to rise into our consciousness.

When Louise is working with clients who repeatedly get stuck in their grieving process, she asks them, *"Who do you cry on?"* Tears shed in isolation are rarely as healing as tears shared with a trusted support person. It is the most beautiful gift we can receive when someone will simply listen without judgment and with compassion to the story of our loss.

For this exchange to be truly effective, we must feel the trustworthiness of the other. We must feel their selfless presence attending our process. They stand with us in the breach, the terrifying gap between what has just transpired and what is yet to come. The healing power of having this witness to our journey cannot be overstated. We will remain numb until we move out of the hollow within ourselves to the embrace of listening hearts.

As women, we are programmed to take care of others and to deny ourselves the recipient role. Every experience of grief, loss, or traumatic change calls us to open and *receive* the care, concern, love, and attention of others. We must, however, actively and courageously *choose* to receive.

Deb's Story

It can be both difficult and very powerful to choose receiving. A few weeks after my mother's passing, Linda phoned and invited me to lunch. As we sat down to lunch she gave me a gift of listening I'll always remember. She had lost her own mother several years before and knew the power of being able to tell the story of your loss. She opened our lunch date by saying, "Tell me about the day your mom died. I want to hear all the details, what happened, how it all unfolded, what you remember most." And then she simply listened.

As I told my story, she carefully and gently asked for even more detail. "What happened after the ambulance came?" "Who did you call from the hospital?" "What else do you remember?" It was her listening that created a new opening into the healing energy of sharing my story and moving forward a tiny bit more from that day's events.

Stories Shared in Community

For women who are used to being independent and in control of things, opening up to the care of others and sharing the story of their grief can be especially challenging. That is because openness implies a certain amount of vulnerability. The reality is that a major loss *does* leave us feeling vulnerable, raw, and exposed. Suddenly we must find new footing in life; we must find yet untapped resources of courage and wisdom to re-shape our days around the emptiness the loss has created in our world. One way to ease the transition from independence to interdependence is through sharing our story with others.

The sharing of our stories with those who are going through similar life passages helps us gain valuable perspective. We tell the story from different angles and as often as needed, until we need to tell it no more. Re-telling the story and being heard, gives us an understanding of the healing quality of time.

Telling the story with siblings, relatives, or other people involved in and affected by the experience can also be revealing and add significantly to our ability to integrate the painful loss. We cannot take everything in nor recall all details when we go through a major loss or trauma. We need the lens that other people offer to build a more complete (and sometimes a more factual) picture.

In ancient traditions, tribal members told their stories around a fire. Individuals heard their own life process reflected through the memories of elders and gained a sense of their place within the communal family history.

In other traditions, women gathered around quilting projects and shared the joys and struggles of human life. Stitched into any quilt would be the stories of grief, sorrow, celebration, and hope that are inevitably part of every woman's story. In a very tangible way, the unbearable became a little more bearable and the hopes and dreams for better tomorrows were supported.

These examples describe a type of sacred community experience that is replicated across the earth perhaps thousands of times every day. In grief support groups, addiction recovery programs, Family Life centers, church gatherings, and even book study clubs, stories are shared and the burden is eased.

By hearing other people's stories you have some way to measure the level of your pain and your recovery process. You listen and absorb hope; you look with softer eyes on where you are at the moment and where you want to be. There is real power in shared experience – it connects with something much larger than your own story, the story of humanity through the ages.

The Strong Emotions of Grief

Our stories of grief and loss are often entwined with deep emotions that are hard to justify and integrate. Feelings of guilt, anger, regret, remorse, frustration, and so many others can sweep through us without a moment's notice. And while they are a natural and normal response to grief, these feelings can also be the first obstacle in our path to healing.

Examples:

- There can be a bittersweet tension between loss and freedom. Sometimes when a loved one dies after an extended illness, one can feel instant relief – a very natural reaction. Then the relief can be followed by an immediate sense of guilt. You are relieved because this person dear to you is no longer suffering. You are also relieved because the tension and stress of caring for them is now lifted from your shoulders. The guilt comes because you feel grateful to be free from the heavy burden and responsibility of care.

• This same kind of tension between conflicting emotions can happen when your life or work circumstances unexpectedly change without your input or control. If you are suddenly laid off or fired from a job, you may feel everything from deep anger and embarrassment to fear or outright panic. You may even feel a guilty sense of reprieve, knowing that even though you won't have income for a while, you could take some down time before looking for the next position.

It is the terrible place of uncertainty in the early stages of grief and loss that can bring out strong emotions. Consider who you might safely talk to about your most intense thoughts and feelings. You want to be able to share them without any concern about being judged and without fear that the listener will try to fix you in some way. Grieving and healing is all a process and it happens more gently within a safe environment.

Grief is never a neat, sequential processing of expected emotions. It is messy. You can feel pretty stable and sure of yourself one minute and completely snowed under the next in a wave of sadness, anger, confusion, or something yet un-namable. And while there are several identifiable stages to the grieving process, they seldom, if ever, pass through in a predictable pattern.

As a minister who has attended many deathbeds and funeral scenes, Louise has often heard women say, "I know I shouldn't feel this way, but…" She tells the grieving ones to immediately let go of the words "should" and "shouldn't" because they are inevitably going to feel a whole range of emotions that are neither good nor bad; they just are. And the emotions felt in the initial days following a loss are bound to resurface a little differently for months yet to come.

Perhaps it is because grief is messy and unpredictable that many people would just rather not deal with it at all. They stuff their feelings, deny them, or try to stomp out their intense feelings through almost manic activity.

Releasing the Guilt

Guilt is a powerful emotion that we can feel in conjunction with grief. It can strike to the core of our relationships. We may feel there was something more we could have or should have done to prevent or alter the ultimate outcome. "If only I had…" "If only I had remembered to say…" "If only I had known…" These or similar punishing thoughts may continue to haunt you until you address them head on. Most of the time in life, the facts stay the same no matter what we could or would have said or done differently.

Guilt and anger are often tightly entwined emotions in the bereavement process.

While you are relieved that the person you loved is no longer suffering, you may also be angry that they didn't take better care of themselves and/or respond sooner to physical warning signals. While you may understand why your company is downsizing and therefore eliminating positions, you can feel personally attacked by their decision to eliminate you. While you may feel gratitude for an inheritance, you may also feel angry and burdened by the new responsibilities placed on you as a steward of that wealth or property.

> Deb's mom smoked for fifty years before she died of lung cancer. Nothing Deb could have said or done would have changed her mother's decision to time and again light up. So nothing Deb could have done would have made a life-altering impact.

In bereavement we look back at things from a very different perspective, and it can be tempting to think that we could have somehow altered the outcome by our own actions or intervention. The fact is that we are not responsible for the actions and choices of others. We are not responsible for someone else's drinking, smoking, drugging, over-eating, or other self-destructive behaviors.

To heal, you must eventually realize that your loved one, in living their own life, may have made decisions that you would prefer they hadn't. Nothing can be done about that now, and probably nothing could have been done then to make a significant change. Let yourself off the hook of this kind of guilt and just be present with your sadness. Keeping yourself on the hook of guilt cannot serve you in any way.

Speaking About Your Anger

There are so many losses that we have to face in life on earth. Some happen through death, some through natural disasters, some through economic downturns, and some through our own choices. Anger can be one of our strongest reactions to change and loss. It is, unfortunately, an emotion that our culture too often denies as a natural human response and so demands that we repress it. This is especially true for women; we seem to find it much easier to express our sadness than to even acknowledge our anger. After all, the words in the dictionary that define an angry woman are disparaging and demeaning. With the many roles that a woman may hold in grieving, it may seem easier to just put her own feelings on the back burner in order to attend to the needs of others.

Some people feel it is spiritually unacceptable to be angry, particularly if that anger is directed toward God. We may be furious that a loved one has been taken from us, yet feel we have no right to question God's Will. Again, it is important to remember that we have a right to ALL of our feelings, no matter what they are. And certainly the Creator, above all others, understands our reactions.

Because of this deeply ingrained and confusing perception we have of anger, we can all greatly benefit from finding a safe place to express it. Talking with a bereavement coach or counselor, a clergy person, or a trusted friend can act like a release valve for the steam of our anger. We need to talk about the facts involved in our loss in order to have a clearer picture of what has happened to us.

If you cannot immediately identify a safe way to express your anger with another, try one of these options:

- Ask yourself who you are angry with or what you are angry about. Write out everything you are thinking and feeling in a journal or write a letter to the person involved, even if that person is no longer alive. Hold nothing back. Use your pen to scream and vent.

• Pound a pillow on your bed and yell. Let go of the frustration that has been building inside you. Be sure that no one else is around so you can freely vent.

• Work up a good sweat at your favorite gym or through working around your house. Do something very physical that will allow the energy of anger to flow through your body and be released.

Speaking about and venting intense emotions helps clear the mental space for reframing our experiences of loss. By acknowledging and addressing these challenging emotions, we make room in our mind and heart for the possibility of tenderness, mercy, forgiveness, and hope.

Letting Go of Pain Echoes

Any new loss can echo back into other losses in life. Unattended grief from the past compounds and complicates a new experience of grief. This is why it is essential for us to take care of old wounds and gradually let go of the past. At some point the re-telling of painful stories, where healing is *not* taking place, begins to build negative energy and a kind of emotional prison.

We don't usually recognize that what we are feeling as we stumble through the first days and weeks after a loss can be something deeper – an echo from a previous, unattended and unhealed trauma. Our culture does not honor the bereavement process, rushing us through it, demanding that we just somehow whip ourselves back into shape and keep going. Given this expectation, it is easy to deny, stuff, or skim over our true feelings.

It takes a conscious choice to move beyond old hurt. Please do not let these echoes of past hurt remain hidden. If your present circumstances reveal old wounds, you have an opportunity to mend these scarred places in your soul now. By dipping back and attending to historical losses, you become stronger than ever before; you reduce their power to cause you pain, you make room for light and new growth, and you weave together your many experiences into a tapestry of new life wisdom.

Reframing the Experience

Telling and retelling stories of grief and loss provides an important outlet for naming and claiming the experience in its entirety. Grief experiences can be too shattering or overwhelming to be absorbed at the time of their happening. Others come to us as gradual processes, extended through lengthy illnesses or as shifts created by an empty nest, the loss of a job or career or through a divorce. Authentic grieving calls the griever into different experiences of the loss over time.

The differing responses you have *are* the reframing of your grief story. Telling and retelling the story, hearing it told by siblings or other loved ones who have been on the journey with you, crying out your sadness – all of these bring new light into your grieving. The intensity of the experience softens. You will be able to see it with new eyes and insights that can inform the choices you make now.

Reflection, the sharing of your story and the subsequent insights you come to, help you gain meaning from your loss over time. This process of reframing enables you to be present to the grief in new ways, taking from it what is needed, learning, growing into the experience and then beyond it. Other life-grief experiences will bring on further reflection, opportunities for reclaiming and releasing what is most and least important about the experiences.

Healing is present in each opportunity of telling your story. Seeing the story differently helps you understand what has been lost and what may be gained. Eventually, the story of your grief will have less power, less control over your emotions, and you will actually arrive in a place of healing and acceptance.

GENTLE REMINDERS

Grief is a whole-person experience. It can impact you on every level of your being – physical, mental, emotional, spiritual.

- For a time you may feel as though you are walking through a dense fog. Know that this will eventually lift.

- Be patient and compassionate with yourself; demand nothing of yourself for a while and let go of all self-criticism.

- Talk to someone you trust about all that you are thinking and feeling. "Tell your story" as many times as you need to.

- Remember that this is a very trying time. Hold on to all the people, activities, and familiar routines that help you feel grounded.

- Allow yourself to have the full range of your emotions without resisting. Notice what you feel and let the feelings pass through you.

- Give yourself permission to receive the love and care of others during this time. Release any compulsion to take care of everyone and everything else.

Coaching Yourself through the Early Stages of Grief

In the early days of grieving, you have less tolerance, lower energy, and your skin may even feel very thin. This is a time for extreme self-care and gentleness. Do not put expectations on yourself, but rather, allow the days to flow with soft and compassionate ease. Here are a few things you can do to walk tenderly through this difficult time:

- *Be very honest about your energy levels,* both with yourself and around others. Do not try to be brave; just be with whatever you are sensing and thinking in the moment. Do not force yourself to do anything that feels beyond your capacity right now. Just do the bare minimum for a while. Gradually your strength will return.

- *Recognize that you have been changed in some way forever.* You will never be able to turn back the clock on this experience. You have been through something very traumatic and it will take time to integrate the pieces of this trauma and decide how to move forward.

- *Be patient.* Some day-to-day decisions may feel overwhelming; other big decisions that appear to be looming may need more time in order for you to gather clarity and advice from others. Just stay quietly open to the unfolding.

SACRED RITUALS
for
Releasing Stories of Pain

"Rituals are internal rites of passage that can revitalize our beliefs and attitudes and give fresh meaning to our lives at a time when meaning has been taken from us. Rituals can help us focus on what is and what can be, rather than what was. They can enhance our expectations and set into motion new beginnings."

– Dr. Catherine M. Sanders, *Surviving Grief*

NOTE:

Rituals have always been an important component of celebrations in the human experience. Whether they are founded on religious, cultural, or secular practices, rituals that are used around the healing of our grief offer us a very tangible expression for our deepest thoughts and feelings. They bring an element of tradition to our bereavement process; they provide a framework for the release of our sorrow. Because of their intrinsic power and value, we include suggested rituals at the end of each chapter in this book.

1. Consider keeping a journal in which you document your grieving process. Be sure to let out all your feelings onto these pages

without holding anything back. This is not the place to worry about grammar, spelling, or proper vocabulary. It is a sacred receptacle for your honest thoughts and your deepest emotions. Imprinting the pages through writing or drawing brings a very real release by moving the energy of pain out of your body.

2. Allow your tears to flow. Tears release toxins from the body, and they are a perfect way to let off the "steam" of emotions.

3. Meditate. Sit in the quiet; breathe deeply; allow everything to be still within you. Open your mind and heart and soul to the healing Voice of Spirit. Just be, and know that you are loved. Receive the grace of the stillness. Everything will be okay.

CHAPTER TWO

Resting in the Unknown

"Close your eyes and softly sigh into the silence. If there is background noise, listen to the silence between sounds. Concentrate on your heart and follow a welcoming pathway deep into it. In peace-filled solitude, drink in the stillness of your soul."

– Sue Patton Thoele, *The Woman's Book of Soul*

Carol's Story

On September 11, 1991, my ex-husband hung himself. Tom suffered from chronic depression, and I'm sure he held on as long as he could. In spite of his difficulties, he was my best friend and the love of my life. Our boys were five and almost seven when he died. Trying to feel my way through my own process and help the kids with theirs at the same time was a challenge. I couldn't tell whose grief was whose…really, it just made me feel insane.

Everyone's grief was different. My five-year-old fell apart, cried himself to sleep, wanted his daddy, asked unanswerable questions, and became terrified of storms and bad weather. My seven-year-old shut down immediately, never shed a tear, refused to admit any feelings at all, and became angry and uncooperative at every opportunity. As for me, I tried to stay in control during the day — I continued to work, dealt with child care, and handled the massive paperwork created by unexpected death. Then when the day was over, I went to my room and cried in isolation. I rode the waves as they came and didn't sleep much.

I couldn't shake the feeling that when Tom died, he took my history with him. No one else knew me intimately, shared the memories of our young life together, the birth of our babies, and all the private jokes and moments. No one else loved my kids the way I did. The loneliness was overwhelming.

Whenever we experience some trauma in life, it is important to know that it affects us on all levels. We need time to rest before pushing forward again. This leg of the journey through grief and loss is perhaps the most challenging. We may find ourselves experiencing the push/pull dynamic of wanting to urgently fill the emptiness in our lives with anything, just to make the pain go away. At the same time, we are torn by feelings of resistance and loyalty to hold on to what once was our reality.

It is so uncomfortable and unfamiliar to be in the "not yet" – the place of unknowing, the mysterious and murky shadow-land of uncertainty. Trying to too quickly get out of the discomfort can sabotage real healing and the potential for healthy new beginnings.

Facing the Loneliness

Everything changes with a major loss or a death in the family. There is an emptiness that no one else will ever be able to fill. Learning to just *be* in that loneliness will take time and courage. It is almost like the phantom pain of an amputation. You turn a corner in your house expecting to see that person; you see someone ahead of you in line who has the same haircut as your loved one. Perhaps you must now sleep alone or figure out all the details of family finances by yourself. Perhaps you have no one to call, where before your loved one was the first person you thought of.

Grief brings many forms of loneliness, and they all offer opportunities for attention. There may be a feeling of being isolated from others in your grief, or the keen awareness of the loss of daily companionship. A rhythm of life has been dramatically interrupted. You may feel lonely at the realization that you face the future alone or without that familiar "other" to share decisions. Hundreds of big and small choices have to be considered, and you may now have to make them all by yourself.

As you look around, you may get the impression that other people are still moving along and going ahead in their lives while you appear to have stalled. Some people who have been impacted by the same loss still seem able to cope and engage each day while you remain frozen. Your sense of isolation then increases as others move on.

Perhaps the deepest loneliness is that no one else really knows exactly how it feels inside of you. Even though others may be grieving the same loss around you, your experience is still different because you are a unique human being. This place of personal numbness and isolation is the very place where God's grace and loving presence can bring a measure of comfort.

Receiving Support

At every stage of the grieving process it is important to keep some connection to trusted others. You need their love, care, support, and unconditional acceptance. Just having someone to listen and hear where you are at any given moment can be deeply healing. Knowing that you are not alone in your journey will invite slow and gentle movement through the difficult hours and days of bereavement.

Carol

I have never been comfortable with public grief. I hate the idea of being a victim so I kept my feelings to myself as much as possible. I don't recommend this. Without support and comfort from others, it's hard to keep moving. You need to tell someone your secrets. Let someone know how you are feeling, when you don't feel like you can go on, and how mad you are. Legitimate grief should be witnessed and validated so you can move past it and get back to living in gratitude and joy.

As we hear in Carol's story, "legitimate grief" calls for companionship. It cannot be traversed alone and unattended. Even while you take the much-needed time in the quiet of your own mind, you also need the input of loving witnesses. Think of this as beautiful balance – the balance between hibernating in your pain and allowing gracious care to touch you.

We have in our culture the idea that it is a personal weakness to receive or to be in need. But at this time in your life, in your grief, you are allowed to be the receiver. Let go of any need to hold it all together and be open to receiving hugs, kind words, or the simple outreach of someone's care. Take a moment to consider where you can go to be in the company of caring friends. Even if you do not have the energy to stay long or to engage in activities, showing up creates the opening for receiving encouragement and support from others.

Filling the Void

There is a tension between moving too quickly and not moving at all when we are grieving, between noticing and allowing the void and doing almost anything to stop the pain within it. It is imperative to just observe ourselves for a while, trusting that the way through will eventually become clear.

When you are in the void, consider trying these self-soothing practices:

- Take a warm shower or bath
- Go for a walk and observe nature
- Sit on a swing in the park
- Breathe consciously
- Listen to music
- Light a scented candle
- Write in your journal
- Look at pictures
- Put on a comforting piece of jewelry or clothing
- Make yourself a cup of tea

Engage yourself in simple, nurturing, calming activities; give yourself permission to just be where you are. Writing in a journal, pouring out onto its open and nonjudgmental pages all the agony of your grieving heart, may be the place to begin. This daily exercise can help you release yet unvented emotions and make room for grace.

If the void feels just too intense and loneliness is flooding your whole being, think of going to a yoga class or some other activity that will help you engage through your body. Physical movement will release clogged energy and free you to feel a little more lightness or joy. A massage can also help to move and release negative energy built up through grief. Tears may come and it is good to just let them flow. It is okay to cry; it is a necessary part of bereavement.

It will be important at this stage of your healing to not demand too much of yourself or to force any action. Balance is the great equalizer in life and within our being. You will want to experiment and see what involvement feels right for you. Don't try to fill the void all at once or with any one activity. Sometimes you must sit in the void for a while to hear your own call for what is needed next.

Resting in the Familiar

Other ways to soothe yourself are to be in a familiar environment, to slowly re-engage in a piece of a daily routine, or to simply hold in your hands objects that have a connection to memories and that give you comfort. This could include wearing a belonging of your loved one, cooking their favorite food so those recognizable smells surround you, listening to music you once shared with that person, going through photo albums, even creating a small altar with images and belongings that you cherish and that are connected with that person. However you decide to wrap yourself in the familiar, know that it is a temporary resting place.

It is tempting for some people to just walk completely away from the familiar and disconnect from it as soon as possible, as if this will stop the pain they are experiencing. It does not; we take the pain of loss with us wherever we go until we turn directly into it and invite healing. Let the familiar be your friend; let it soothe you and calm you whenever possible. The time for moving on comes soon enough.

THE SWEATER - *A Story from Louise*

I loved my father-in-law very much. He was a true gentleman and an intelligent, gentle, kind-hearted man. In many ways it was easier for me to love him than it had been to love my own father. So when Lester died very suddenly of a stroke, I was incredibly sad. It was as if a light had gone out not only in our family but in my own heart as well.

My husband had the responsibility of going through his parents' home and deciding how all their things would be dispersed. One day I was helping him with this task and, for some reason, I latched onto Dad's old brown cardigan. It was one of those classic sweaters with leather patches at the elbows and a v-neck front with five buttons.

For almost a year that simple piece of clothing was a touchstone of my memories and my grief. I wore it with everything and anything that its color and style would remotely co-ordinate with. And sometimes I wore it just to feel his loving presence around me again.

One day I knew it was time to let that sweater go, and I placed it in a box to a local charity. My father-in-law is long gone from the earth, the sweater is no longer in my possession, but the memories of our relationship are with me forever.

Making Room for Silence

As you begin to feel and process the pain of your loss, the perfect place to rest in the unknown can often be the silence within. Author Sue Patton Thoele describes it this way in *The Woman's Book of Soul*:

> *Close your eyes and softly sigh into the silence. If there is background noise, listen to the silence between sounds. Concentrate on your heart, and follow a welcoming pathway deep into it. In peace-filled solitude, drink in the stillness of your soul.*

It is so easy to overlay the intense emotions of grief with the noise of the world in an attempt to smother them. The incessant chatter of radio or TV, attendance at loud events or large group gatherings, talking mindlessly on the phone, or sitting numbly for hours in front of a computer screen – all of these are merely distractions from what really needs your attention.

Our culture encourages us to continue to push forward as if nothing has dramatically changed in our lives. After suffering a major loss, it is not the time to force a "normal" routine. It is essential to give ourselves permission to take care of ourselves first, wherever we are in the moment. Creating the space and time for silence can be a form of sanctuary that soothes the tender places within you, allowing you to gradually find comfort and healing.

Consider these three ways to enter into silence:

1. If you find your sleep interrupted, get up. Get out of bed and find a quiet place to sit with your journal. Resist the temptation to turn on lights, instead enjoying the ambient light of the night. Listen and let yourself be cradled in the comforting, familiar sounds of your home or back yard.

2. Think of a place you can go that doesn't cost any money – perhaps the grounds of a museum or city park. Resist the urge to take an iPod or talk to someone on the phone. Walk *slowly*, find quiet places to sit, observe and listen. Notice birds, water sounds, trees, plants, and other people going by. Just be!

3. Visit chapels and sanctuaries in your community. Most are open throughout the day with little activity. These are beautiful places to sit by yourself, allow your memories and tears to flow, and soak up the faith of the ages.

Silence can be immediately calming and soothing, something needed almost moment to moment in times of sorrow and adjustment. During bereavement many people notice they have a much lower tolerance for noise, crowds, certain smells, anything that seems to *assault* their senses. This is because we wear our nerve endings so close to the surface in grief and our usual everyday defenses are weakened. In fact some people even experience susceptibility to illness during this time.

As you allow the stillness of nature or of your own breath and heartbeat to soothe you, you are actually practicing a form of meditation. Here in the quiet, the Divine can touch you and lift you above the pain of grief into glimpses of hope. In the silence within, God can speak to your heart and fill you with loving comfort.

Learning To Say No

While there can be a strong pull of habit in you to take care of others, bereavement is a time for *radical* self-care! So it is very important to guard this time and to set good boundaries. There is no one right way or one perfect time schedule for grieving, and you can take all the time needed to honor your own process.

Some people may reach out to us when we are down and try to engage us in activities that we are just not ready for. While they are well meaning, we need to give ourselves permission to evaluate each offer and to clearly state our preference. It may be hard to trust our intuitive sense of what would be good for us, especially in the face of someone else's measure of where we "should" be in our process. "Shoulding" on ourselves is a form of subtle abuse and a discount of our own needs.

Consider this example:

If you have agreed to a business or social activity, and upon arriving find you just do not have the inner stamina to follow through, give yourself permission to leave. You can simply say to those involved, "I'm not ready for this today." You can also suspend your decision. Rather than immediately declining an invitation, ask if you can give your answer closer to the scheduled event. This gives you time to perhaps feel a little stronger.

Saying "no" may not be in your nature; you may have been raised to believe that you must always keep the peace and make others comfortable. But this is a time to consider *first* your own comfort by giving yourself permission to respond differently. Take your time; read your body; be okay with other people's discomfort. You are not responsible for the world. You are responsible for your own wellbeing.

Assessing Your Readiness

Your readiness to engage in life is going to be different each day. Please read this first statement again and put it on a post-it note if you need to. Get it deep into your consciousness, because your healing depends on it. Some days you may have a high energy level and at other times, feel you have no energy at all, especially when it involves interacting with others.

You may find that family members and friends feel uncomfortable seeing you in pain. They may try to "fix" your pain by pressing you into activity.

Trust your own intuition about whether you feel up to participating or not. Be firm in stating your preference, allowing yourself to accept or decline.

This is no time to worry about someone else's emotional reaction to you. This is not the time to take care of other people's feelings or expectations. This is YOUR time to rest in the unknown, to pay attention to your own needs, and to gently move into healing.

Carol

Grief led me to a life of gratitude and acceptance. I now know that I have to appreciate everything and expect nothing. I also learned that helping others when I'm at my worst can be the thing that saves me from self-destruction. Wallowing in self-pity is not legitimate grieving. Everyone experiences loss at some point. Grief is the process we use to grow through it and learn from it. So my advice is to feel it deeply, scream and cry and laugh and stomp your feet, because the only way out is facing it head on.

GENTLE REMINDERS

• During bereavement you may need much more rest than you normally do. When you feel tired, take a nap if that is an option. Follow the leading of your body.

• Loneliness is often a companion to grief. Honor your need for quiet and alone time, yet monitor yourself so you do not slip into extended isolation.

• Intentional times of silence can be tremendously healing, especially if you connect these times to prayer, meditation, or other sacred ritual.

• The familiar can also be soothing to your soul during this time. Let the sights, sounds, tastes, and smells of the familiar fill your senses and hold you in their healing friendship.

• Pay attention to your fluctuating energy levels; only participate in events and activities when you feel strong enough to engage. Say "no, thank you" to invitations that you are not yet ready for.

• This is a time to guard your heart and your whole being by putting yourself and *your* needs first.

Coaching Yourself through the Unknown

The human heart is a delicate instrument that pumps life-giving blood through the body, and it is also a powerful receptacle for all the emotions you will experience in bereavement. You may find yourself energetically challenged for a long time as you integrate the layers of your grief. This is a time of life for attending to your physical and emotional needs. Guard your heart during these initial days of uncertainty by considering the following ways to support your healing:

- **Learn to do a self-check** before accepting any invitation. Give yourself permission to delay your response; "I'd like to check my schedule and get back to you," is an acceptable reply. Check in with yourself to see if you feel you have enough energy to participate at this time. Learning to do a self-check can help you determine what feels best.

- **Develop an exit strategy** for situations in which you may feel overwhelmed or drained of energy. If you find yourself in a meeting, social gathering, or other public event and realize it is just too much, give yourself permission to leave. Radical self-care means having the courage and boundaries to put yourself first.

- You are in the space of "not-yet-right," a place of uncertainty in which you may need more quiet time and down time than you are used to allowing. **Honor the intuitive call for stillness, aloneness, and self-soothing.** Taking care of your own needs will bring the next measure of healing.

SACRED RITUALS
for
Resting in the Unknown

1. **Walk a labyrinth.** Check in your area for indoor and outdoor labyrinths. Some will even provide a short history and description of how to use this ancient walking meditation. This experience will help you calm the inner noise and enter healing silence.

2. **Choose a familiar object** such as a piece of clothing, a jewelry item, a favorite photograph, or any other memento and spend some time in the quiet with this touchstone. Allow your memories; allow your tears; stay open to insights that may come as you hold this item close to your heart.

3. **Create an altar.** Place on your altar objects that have deep meaning for you and that connect you to your loved one and your spiritual practice. Keep the altar small and be reflective about how the objects you choose may change over time.

CHAPTER THREE

Respecting Your Own Process

"Another factor that causes grief to be painful is that…we lack social supports that offer us comfort and nurturance…. We are expected to disguise our pain, hide our emotions, and keep a controlled demeanor lest we make others feel uncomfortable."

– Dr. Catherine M. Sanders,
Surviving Grief…and Learning to Live Again

Grief and loss bring out the best and worst in most of us. They pull from our soul great courage and unexpected strength to go on in the face of sorrow; they pull from our ego resistance to change; they can stir in us the strongest feelings and emotions we have ever had. The process of grieving, then, is almost a reflection of the shadow self and the light that is within each psyche.

Because grief is such a personal experience, you should never compare your bereavement process to anyone else's. You are bound to have some predictable reactions and also to find yourself embroiled in unexpected and unpleasant responses. It is important to release yourself from any internal judgment about your emotions. Everything you feel in reaction to grief and loss is real, valid, and worthy of your attention.

Anger, Sadness, and Guilt

In our society, women are still too often denied the honest expression of their anger. Some feel they cannot vent their anger unless they can prove that it is somehow "justified." Perhaps they have already experienced the repercussions of a loved one's rebuke when they have tried to speak about their anger. Some have even been labeled "bitch" or other derogatory terms. It is no surprise then that many women have grown into adulthood suppressing this natural human emotion and burying it under the cover of something else. There are, unfortunately, several consequences to long-hidden and long-denied angers.

At womenhealthandbeauty.com, a 2009 article on anger and grief stated:

> *We can pretend anger is not there, not let it out. But it roils beneath the surface still. It does tremendous damage to our physical well being. It gains strength with time. It changes our personality and our social abilities. It becomes depression. It becomes fuel for addiction and abuse.*

Denied and suppressed anger can also be the underlying cause of sleep disturbances, tension headaches, anxiety disorders, and other debilitating health issues. Women who do not allow themselves the healthy expression and release of their anger stay stuck in negative grief cycles longer than those who honor their true feelings. For them, sadness can become their default emotion. All anger, then, begins to feel like sadness, weighing them down and keeping them emotionally stuck.

Along with the problem of not being able to express anger effectively, some women have the mistaken belief that to show their *sadness* is tantamount to being a whining or complaining person that no one wants to be around. It is true that whining is not appreciated, but the sincere release of one's deep sorrow is an absolutely necessary step in re-claiming inner peace and balance. Sadness, like all strong emotions, can be eased by sharing it with more than one person. You won't wear that one person out if you use a whole support network.

Knowing the difference between your anger and your sadness is important because it allows you to better articulate what you are going through. Making the distinction between these emotions can help you take appropriate action in support of your own healing. When the two remain enmeshed, it is much more difficult to release either one of them and move forward.

Kellie's Story

Brittany and I met the summer before my seventh grade and her sixth grade year. Her family moved into an old house two doors from me. She was a year younger than me but that made no difference. Since that day I have never found a closer friend. From giggly sleepovers to high school heartbreaks, we laughed and cried together while we watched each other grow up. When I moved away to college she stayed in our hometown about an hour away.

One day I received a devastating phone call while enjoying a pleasant lunch by myself in my crowded dorm cafeteria. I was between classes at Michigan State University, and the mutual friend who made the call did not prepare me for the news she was about to break. I remember her vividly telling me that Brittany had hung herself and hearing this weird whooshing noise in my ears. I'm not sure what my immediate reply was, but I know that at the time, I thought that Britt was in the hospital.

When my best friend took her life I experienced the most painful heartbreak I could have imagined and more. I went through every stage of grief I had learned about in high school psychology, without even realizing it at the time. I denied that she was gone. I was so angry with her for inflicting such pain on all those who loved and continue to love her so much. I stood next to her casket

screaming at her in my head, "THIS IS SO STUPID!
Just dumb!" I bargained, wished, and I begged whoever
God is for the whole experience to be only a dream. I was
willing to do anything to have my best friend and closest
confidant back...and then, I was just plain sad.

Identifying Your True Feelings

What does anger feel like to you?

Are you able to recognize some physical change in
your body when you get angry, irritated, frustrated, or
upset? You may want to develop a practice of checking
in with your body periodically to gauge what you are
really feeling. Here are several anger responses that
women report feeling:

- tight shoulders
- tense stomach muscles
- shallow breathing
- clenched jaw or hands
- restlessness and inability to sit still
- a generalized feeling of being on edge
- an urge to release the pent-up energy through
  some physical action

Anger in bereavement is often about the lack of control, the sense of powerlessness over the loss or trauma you have experienced. It is frequently enmeshed with other strong emotions such as guilt, shame, and fear. It is essential, therefore, to give yourself permission to sort through your feelings so you know what you are really dealing with at that moment.

If anger is not dealt with, it can come out in inappropriate ways. You could find yourself wanting to rage at some innocent bystander, such as the unsuspecting auto repair person or an individual in front of you in a long line at the grocery store. The urge to drive recklessly, slam doors, or kick the cat may all be indicative of unattended anger. Just about anyone could become your scapegoat for this suppressed emotion.

What does sadness feel like to you?

As women, we often want to protect others from our true feelings and give the impression that we are holding things together. Somehow this seems to be the image we are supposed to project to society. It is no wonder, then, that it is so hard to distinguish our true emotions. For many women, sadness may have similar qualities or characteristics to their sense of anger. If this is true for you, you will need to check in with your body to see what you are really experiencing. Common indicators of sadness include:

- frequent crying spells
- physical heaviness
- general malaise
- the tendency to isolate oneself
- mood swings
- short-term memory loss or the inability to stay focused

The sadness we experience after a loss is not something that is going to go away quickly. It can stay with us for years, even a lifetime, as in the case of a parent who has lost a child. But sadness should never be allowed to alter our personality or limit our personal or professional growth.

We don't want to let our anger or sadness become the driving force of our identity. When addressed with care and compassion, these emotions can be absorbed into the very fiber of our being and integrated into our life as new strength.

What does guilt feel like to you?

Elisabeth Kubler-Ross, author of ground-breaking work on death and dying, once said, *"Guilt is perhaps the most painful companion of death."* Guilt over a loss or death can take many forms. It can come as a result of unfinished business with someone who has passed or from the sense that we could have handled things differently. It is often accompanied by self-judging thoughts such as, "If I had only said or done…" "If only I had responded sooner." "If only I could have seen this coming."

Guilt may show up in any of the following ways:

- regrets
- obsessive thoughts
- hyper-vigilance around unrelated things
- a compulsive need to resolve the irresolvable
- an unrealistic desire to go back in time and change things
- harsh self-judgment and criticism

As with anger or sadness, unresolved guilt weakens a person's normal defenses and can even result in self-abusive behaviors. Please seek immediate professional assistance if you notice a tendency to want to harm yourself in any way during your bereavement process.

Since guilt seems to be an unavoidable response to loss, when you notice guilty feelings, you should view them as an opportunity to practice self-compassion instead of self-judgment. Being compassionate means that you can step back from the situation, observe your responses, and then let them go. Hanging on to guilt does not serve any purpose and certainly does not support healing.

In the bereavement process, guilt gives you a chance to open your heart to the grace of mercy. Forgive yourself for any omission regarding your relationship with the person or situation you are grieving. Forgiveness allows you to see things differently and with a more realistic strategy for moving forward.

Spiritual Anger

A topic too seldom addressed in our society is that of spiritual anger. Many people find themselves furious with God over the death of their loved one or the trauma of some other significant loss. They take the experience very personally, as if it were an intentional act of an authoritative deity aimed directly at them. Or they may feel that their life plans, now suddenly thrown off course, have been sabotaged by an unseen, unfeeling, and punishing power.

For some, the separation from their loved one

or from a desirable situation magnifies a sense of disconnection from Source. They are left without comfort, abandoned, rudderless, and ungrounded with only their pain to accompany them. For others, the sense of rage over the loss is so deep, so profound, that they intentionally distance themselves from their spiritual support.

Spiritual anger can result in a desire to lash out at one's traditions, at those who try to offer comfort from a religious or spiritual perspective, or at the Creator. Just as guilt can be an opportunity for forgiveness, spiritual anger can lead to a re-evaluation of one's beliefs and practices. A much more meaningful relationship with Source and with spiritual community can evolve out of this time of bereavement. Allow your angry, guilty, or sad feelings to come out, address them honestly, and trust that God's love is always bigger than your emotions.

Please be aware that your spiritual life may look completely different on the other side of your grieving. You may find yourself comforted, soothed, and nurtured by unexpected spiritual resources. Keep an open mind and heart and you will come through with new hope.

Respect Your Own Timing

Your bereavement process will take as long as it needs to take, and pieces of it may continue to emerge in years ahead. So, as much as possible, you will need to refrain from comparing your feelings, your grief responses, and your timing to anyone else's. Subsequent losses may bring you back to revisit yet unhealed or unaddressed areas of the loss you are presently grieving. This "bounce-back" grief may come as a surprise to you, but it is a very real and natural part of human growth.

Staying present to your bereavement journey now will serve you in future life experiences. Be patient with yourself; be gentle and kind to yourself; know that your individual process is unique to you and cannot be rushed to suit your own or someone else's agenda. Be open to waiting in the unknown. You can't force your way forward or, through mere thinking, figure out the layers of your grief.

Kellie

As I contemplate my grief journey, I am thinking so hard about what contributed the most to my healing, and I'm still at a loss. Perhaps there has been nothing that has helped me but time, the comfort of talking about my experience of the loss of Brittany with my close friends, and the outreach of my mother. I suppose the only thing I can be sure of is that I am still in the process of healing, still on the road to recovery, still winding my way through the grief journey.

The bubble surrounding me, cutting me off from life, has cleared up and floated away slowly, but the memory of it is still a constant force. The sting of loss still rains down on me with a fury two years later, at times when I least expect it: during the birth of a friend's child, when I glance at the top left window out of habit as I drive past her house, when I hear certain music, and even today as I was washing my face, my shoulders unexpectedly began to shake as I leaned over the sink.

I am confident that the dull throb of loss will always persist in my life, but I have begun to deal with it and hope that some good will eventually come from my painful experiences.

Grieving Multiple Losses

A young woman who had lost her mother, her aunt, and her grandmother all within less than three years, said upon hearing of the sudden death of her uncle, *"I have no room for this."* Her response clearly reflects the overwhelming impact that multiple losses can have upon anyone. If you have not had the time to absorb and process one loss and another quickly follows, you may be left in the tsunami of compounded grief.

There are times and ages in life when one loss or major shift may be followed rapidly by others. In fact, the new loss may trigger a domino effect in which other dramatic changes take place. Even if the changes are consciously chosen, losses may be imbedded within them. All of this begins to build into a raging storm of unprocessed and unhealed emotions. That is why it is so important to learn how to grieve and to attend to your own need for healing all along the journey of life.

Deb's Story

I went through a six-year period in which multiple losses were delivered into my life. It stacked up, compressed, layered, and cut deeply. In that short span I lost my father and mother, a church home, a sense of community, two beloved dogs, my capacity to have children, jobs and career goals and relationships.

My loss experience of grief upon grief casts a long shadow upon all things. In my grief, I have opened myself to noticing, feeling, reflecting on, and crying about the absence of both my beloved parents. I have slowly learned to live without the dialogue of their presence in my everyday life. In their passing, I have also lost the center of my family.

A mere five months after my father's passing, I had to have a hysterectomy. It was the end of any dream of having children of my own. I felt hollowed out by this loss, completely gutted physically and emotionally by the combination of these two traumas. Three months after this surgery, my husband and I decided to return to our home state to be near my mother. We sold our house and left behind our treasured church family and long-term friendships that were the anchors of our everyday life. In this move, we both gave up careers and all the relationships associated with them.

Eighteen months after our return to Indiana, my mother died. My sisters and I were left orphans, responsible for dealing with my parents' home and fifty years of accumulated belongings. In the midst of these losses, I also experienced the death of two dear pets, companions of my life.

What I've learned through all this is that everything changes. Nothing, **nothing** stays the same. The losses are all linked together and could, if I let them, become the foundation for defining who I am. Instead, though, I choose for them to be passages of my life. I have tried to actively face these traumatic, multiple changes — naming them, assigning them to their place in my overall journey, and honoring even the deepest losses within the layers of the many.

While I was in the middle of all of these losses, I was not always aware of how huge they were. I needed the voices of others to validate the depth of my own pain. One of my friends reminds me still, "You are not where you were." What this means to me is that I am moving forward, even if it doesn't feel like it.

Layers of Grief Support

We need other people to ground us and support us through the life-altering layers of our bereavement. From grief support groups to the simple exchange with a friend, life offers us healing opportunities in many forms. Each one and all of them can be the difference between being swallowed up in our pain or rising above it.

In the beginning stages of your grief, it may feel almost impossible to talk to others about what you are going through. You may feel disconnected, speechless, and totally unprepared for the waves of unfamiliar emotions that assault you. It may be difficult to determine what is normal and what is totally out of line. Grief coaches, bereavement counselors, grief support groups, and trusted friends can provide a sage place for releasing your thoughts and feelings. They can validate your process and give insight into healthy ways to walk through the days of darkness and confusion.

As you move along through the stages of grieving, you may find the need for different kinds of support. You may need the comfort of familiar faces early on and then need the fresh perspective of total strangers later, as in a support group. What you are looking for is confirmation of your process. Those who have experienced losses similar to yours can offer unique and valuable insight that can encourage you and help you gauge your progress.

Finding Laughter in the Pain

In her book, *The Song of the Seed, A Monastic Way of Tending the Soul*, author Macrina Wiederkehr says:

> *The most helpful discovery of today has been that right in the midst of my sorrows there is always room for joy. Joy and sorrow are sisters; they live in the same house.*

Many people report feeling embarrassed or uneasy when they burst into laughter while planning a funeral, as if somehow they need to maintain a more somber demeanor. Yet laughter and tears are mirror images of life and they both offer release of emotion. They are both valid expressions of grieving.

The truth is that humor often heals. Stories shared around a dinner table after someone's passing can ignite a storm of memories. Some of those memories will elicit an eruption of laughter, allowing bubbles of healing energy to fill the room. Sometimes giggles will dissolve back into tears, and again, there is a release. There is no need for self-judgment or judgment of others about the appropriate way to grieve. Grief is a complex and multi-layered process that moves one to feel the widest range of emotions. Joy and sorrow walk hand in hand; they need each other; they knit together the positive and negative aspects of human life.

You will show up in your grief, just as you are at that moment, as will everyone else around you. You will cry, laugh, be angry, be silent, feel confused or lost, ask questions, and everything in between. That is the journey of bereavement.

GENTLE REMINDERS

• Bereavement is often a time of intense emotions. Trying to block your honest feelings will interfere with the healing process. Pay attention to your emotions. Give them expression.

• Notice how your body informs you of your feelings, how it gets your attention. Persistent body discomfort can indicate blocked emotions or toxic energy you need to address. Seek professional help to assist you in making an evaluation of what is needed. (Be cautious about medicating your emotions. Find appropriate and healthy ways to process them instead.)

• Remember to reach out for any and all support you need during your bereavement.

• Never compare yourself and your way of grieving with anyone else's. Grief is an intensely personal process. There is no one "right" way to find comfort and healing. Learn what works for you and honor it.

Coaching Yourself through Your Own Process

As you go through the journey of grief and reach for healing of your pain, you are bound to experience big swings in your emotions. In this chapter, we explored the importance of honoring and respecting your own needs, your own timing, and your own individual responses.

- *What are you feeling at this moment about the loss you have experienced?* Use your journal to report these feelings and consider sharing them with someone you trust. Getting your emotions out onto a written page moves them out of your body to a place where you can look at them more objectively.

- *How is your spiritual life being affected by your grief?* Consider speaking with your clergy person, spiritual coach, or grief counselor to further explore and resolve any conflicts in this area.

- *Are you finding yourself dealing with a health issue in your bereavement?* This could be an indication that suppressed emotions such as anger, sadness, or guilt need to be expressed. Give yourself permission to feel everything. It may also be a time to check in with your regular physician and make sure everything is okay.

SACRED RITUALS
for
Respecting Your Own Process

The emotions that are attached to grief and loss can be held inside for many years. Holding on to these feelings is a way of keeping the trauma alive, giving it power over progress in life. Rituals of release really honor your process and give you a tangible way to respectfully let go of the past and the pain.

1. If you find yourself with unresolved anger, sadness, or guilt, write a letter to the person you are most upset with at this time. This is a letter that you do not send; it is simply for the purpose of venting your honest emotions. Say whatever you need to say. Talk about the things that are still standing between you and a little peace of mind. Then burn this letter in a simple prayerful ceremony, letting go of every difficult feeling.

2. In all spiritual traditions there are writings that reflect humanity's struggle with and longing for the Divine. Seek out sacred texts, current spiritual writings, poetry, music, or stories that help you reconnect with your

soul and with your Maker. Open yourself to being comforted spiritually, to being guided from within, and to the loving touch of life.

CHAPTER FOUR

Redefining Who You Are Now

"...I realized that it's not always about survival, this life we are given; it's usually so much easier than that. It's about trusting the eternal life force that is flowing within us — letting that force lead the way through all the inevitable changes we will face across the span of our time here on Earth."

— Elizabeth Lesser, *Broken Open:*
How Difficult Times Can Help Us Grow

Pam's Story

My experience of grief and loss has to do with my husband of twenty-eight years. When he was fifty-eight and I was forty-six, he had the option of retiring after thirty-three years of service as an engineer. We were on top of the world, beginning to plan our move back to his home state of New Mexico and looking forward to what we felt would be a rewarding future together.

We had a financial planner helping us to secure our retirement monies and thought we had all of our ducks in a row. Then a few of my husband's very close friends and I began to notice his inability to perform what should have been natural, simple tasks, like turning his computer on, dressing skills, or picking specific items up at the store. It wasn't exactly worrisome yet because, what the hell, we had it all figured out, right? WRONG!

Our trips to several doctors and specialists and lots of testing confirmed a probable diagnosis of early-onset Alzheimer's. How could this be, I thought… We had our future already planned and this did not fit into that plan.

So that takes me to the grieving part. Alzheimer's is something that starts long before the person dies. They may not physically leave you right away, but they do a disappearing act right before your very eyes. I've been told that the name for this type of grieving is "anticipatory grief," meaning you experience someone you love dying over a very long period of time. In my case it was a sixteen year journey; my husband passed away in 2007.

Any major loss can affect your sense of identity. For example, if you lose your job and you have tied your whole life or a good part of it into that work, how do you now define yourself, now that you are no longer employed? If you lose a spouse, you are no longer part of a couple; if you lose a parent or a child, your roles in the family may now change dramatically. This shift in outer circumstances is intimately tied to inner direction.

It is important, then, in the healing process, to recognize this dynamic and to really take the time to honor it. In rethinking your role and identity, there are new opportunities to consciously grow. It is a time to choose a direction that is not tied to your own expectations or those of others who are no longer in your life.

Difficult Questions and Wise Answers

What do you *really want* now? Who do you *really want to be* from this point forward in your life? Where would you *really like to live*? What would you *really enjoy doing*? Who do you *really want to be with*?

These are but a few of the difficult questions that can lead you to amazing growth and self-knowledge after your loss. They are like direction finders, pointing to what would best serve your life now. Just the exercise of asking yourself a question makes room for new information to rise up from within your mind and heart. And there is no need to push yourself into finding the answers quickly, no need to demand that you have them before you begin to move forward.

A better way to answer these reflective questions is to just let the answers find you. Let them slowly come to your conscious mind as you gently go about the process of healing. Trust that the Spirit or your

Higher Self is guiding you and the way is already being prepared for you. Rest into the natural timing of things; it will be perfect for your next steps.

Crossroads of Decision

When you feel a readiness to move forward, to reach out and re-engage in life, you may find that you are facing real turning points. Some things from the past may not feel like they fit any more. Or you may notice yourself being drawn to new experiences, surprising opportunities, and new ways of thinking about yourself. Turning points do not have to be scary; they do not have to be intimidating or threatening. They can be beautiful doors of soul growth.

NEW CAREER PATH: If you have lost a career path or a significant work-life position, you have the opportunity to choose again. Do you really want to stay engaged in this type of employment or are you daring enough to think in a new direction? What are you curious about? Remember to take the fear factor out for a moment and just let your mind play in the field of possibilities.

NEW LIVING ARRANGEMENTS: Major life changes such as an empty nest, the loss of a loved one, divorce, or a natural disaster can invite or force you to choose new living arrangements. Again, this is an opportunity to do some serious thinking – to reflect on what you *really* want from now on. As you are thinking this through, consider the whole environment – the kind of neighborhood energy you want, the type of home or apartment, its proximity to family, amenities, shopping, nature, or your workplace. Think of everything. Make a list of your priorities and preferences.

NEW SUPPORT NETWORK: Sometimes a major loss tips our whole world on end. We may find friendships shifting as some people drift away from us and others draw near. We may notice a need for a new kind of support, as from people who are going through a similar life event. We may notice the need to release the bonds of friendship from those who cannot understand and encourage our growth. This is a time to surround yourself with a community of healthier people. Where will you begin?

NEW FAMILY ROLES: Who are you now if you are no longer someone's spouse, partner, daughter, mother, sister, or relative? Perhaps you have become the sole provider for your family. Or maybe a loss has catapulted you into the role of care-giver who is responsible now for someone else's welfare. Roles may be completely reversed, and you may have to lead family decisions as never before. This may also be a time when you have to make decisions that others will not agree with. Find a strong support person who will help you think things through, always with *your* highest good in mind.

Support for Major Decisions

All of the crossroads of decision mentioned above will ask something new or deeper from you. You will need to make good decisions and take actions that truly reflect your values, purpose, intentions, and preferences. Here are some suggestions of professionals who can support your new choices:

- Grief Coach
- Financial Advisor
- Attorney
- Mediator
- Realtor
- Estate Sale Planner
- Property Manager
- Career Coach or Head Hunter
- Medical Advocate
- Medical Claims Expert

When you are going through the shock waves of a major loss or change, remember that your thinking process is interrupted. This is no time to try to figure everything out by yourself. It's also important to trust your own intuition and not immediately defer to the opinions and ideas of others. If you consult a professional for their advice, give yourself time to integrate that information at your own pace. Ask more questions if you feel uncertain about how to proceed. That is what these qualified experts are there for, answering your questions until you are satisfied.

No matter what your dilemma is about – i.e., selling the family home, moving to a new state, figuring out insurance or other legal papers, making financial decisions you've never made alone – it is a process of discernment. Be patient with yourself and take the time you need.

Perhaps you are caught up in a situation that really does demand immediate decisions that you do not feel prepared to make. Find someone you trust to walk through this process with you or someone who can give you quick advice from their own experience. Even in the demand and rush of needed action, you can reach out for voices of reason and reach within for intuitive guidance.

From Orphan to Elder

Most of us will eventually face the time when we are the elders of our families or communities. Older people before us pass away and we are left to fill their shoes and to take up the mantle of leadership. It can be lonely at first as we begin to realize there is no one ahead of us now who knows the family history. It is now our responsibility. For women, this is particularly important as we are often the "glue" that holds families together.

Who will now identify the images in old photos? Who remembers the recipe for pickling beets? Who will remember to send birthday greetings or anniversary cards? Who knows the story behind that old linen tablecloth or some piece of furniture that has been in the family forever? These are but a few of the *simpler* questions that can haunt us in the absence of our loved ones.

Deeper questions may include:

- Where is my real home?
- What is the shape of our family now?
- Who will remember things if I don't?
- Who will care about our family history if I don't?
- What parts of our family history are essential to pass along?
- What belongings shall I keep to pass on to others?
- What traditions do I want to honor?

As the new family elder, we get to choose what parts of the family knowledge and history we want to hold and treasure. Choices such as this can be very freeing. The answers come over time; they evolve with the passing of days and the grace of small steps. We may be totally unprepared for the transition into the role of elder, so we may need to just do our best right now, knowing we can always make new choices later.

From Couple to Single

We are in a time of living where more than 50% of all marriages end in divorce each year. This staggering figure alone tells us that women are facing the painful transition from being a married partner to single at an amazing rate. Add to this statistic the grief of those who face the death of their spouse through disease, accident, suicide, military service, or natural causes and it is obvious that there is a constant need for healing in the human family.

Sometimes the transition to being a single person again is a chosen path. Sometimes, as stated above, it comes suddenly upon us and leaves us reeling under the weight of a new label, i.e., "widow," "divorcee," "single mother." These labels are not our true identity, yet they do identify in some small measure what we are going through. Remember too that this label is temporary; you will not be identified under it forever. It is not the core of who you are; it is just part of your present journey.

Maybe your spouse was the connector, the one

who was more outgoing and the one who initiated friendships. Perhaps you were part of a circle of married peers and now find yourself on the outside of this familiar group. In the case of a divorce, your friends may feel they have to choose sides and don't know how to remain loyal to both of you. You may feel that you have suddenly become a member of a different club, a club you don't really want to be identified with.

These changes in identity can feel unjustly isolating. They are a very real secondary layer of loss and a legitimate reason to grieve.

From Employee to Job Seeker

Being fired is devastating! Losing your job because of a dramatic downturn in the economy is no less distressing. Most of us need to work; we need the income to care for ourselves and our families. So the sudden loss of employment can throw us into as much of a grief spiral as a death.

Along with losing our job, we lose connections to our fellow employees; we lose a sense of confidence in ourselves as contributors; we lose daily structure to our lives; we lose a place of belonging where others count on us and we count on them. Even leaving a job by choice, but without another position to go to, can cause unexpected sadness and confusion.

Louise's Story

One of the most traumatic events of my life was being fired from a job I desperately needed. I had just separated from my husband and had moved out of state with our two school-aged children. I needed immediate income, so through an agency, I found a management position in women's fashion.

While I was very grateful for this job, I was not in a good frame of mind at the time. I was more traumatized by the breakup of my marriage than I ever let on to anyone and really needed the support and wise counsel of others. Instead I was in a work position where I was the one expected to provide the energy of leadership and vision. Not surprisingly, I began to make little mistakes; my vulnerability began to leak through in conversations with my employers. To add to this tension, I quickly realized that I was really an outsider in a tight, family-run company.

One morning, things came to a head and one of the owners fired me without warning. Needless to say, I was stunned. I needed this job because I needed the income. To fail meant that I might have to move back in with a husband I wasn't sure I could live with any more. The shock waves of being fired, which included some shame and humiliation, were so intense that I don't even remember the half-hour drive home or what I did in the days after. I felt like a complete failure as a wife, a mother, and an employee. My anger, confusion, and sense of self-loathing were so deep, but I didn't know where to turn for help and healing. So I proceeded to get physically sick instead.

Losing a job is no small matter. This kind of identity loss can cut to the core of our sense of self-worth. We can feel completely adrift and judged by those around us who are still employed. Our changing financial condition can feel urgent and out of control. This is a time to seek as much support as possible and to stay open to receiving the help we need.

From Community Member to Anonymous Traveler

Facing displacement, by choice or by outer events, can trigger totally unanticipated grief. Possible circumstances include:

- Retiring
- Moving to a new city
- Moving for a new company or position
- Natural disasters, fire/flood/storm
- Returning to a former community after years away
- Leaving behind community links and connections
- Moving to another country

It is important to recognize that anything which moves us dramatically out of our *usual* and *normal* is bound to create emotional tension which needs to be addressed. It takes so much energy to adjust to new surroundings and find our footing again. It takes time and conscious effort to establish a familiarity with the new environment and to build a trusted network of resources and services.

The quickest way to move through our grief and subsequent emotional turmoil after a major relocation is to claim our new territory as soon as possible. We need to intentionally begin to familiarize ourselves with the neighborhood, the shopping areas, the medical facilities, the available repair services, the public common areas and parks, and so on. The sooner we get out and about in this way, the sooner and more easily the shock waves of the unfamiliar will be absorbed.

Moving Forward

Reassessing and making new choices for your life involves a balancing act between feeling your grief over the changes and finding your way in new situations or settings. If you notice that you do not have a lot of motivation yet to get out and connect, relax and wait for a better time. Be gentle with yourself always, honoring that you have an ebb and flow of energy each day.

Taking the first tentative steps to redefining who you are now is a courageous act. It takes time to make life-altering decisions. Some days you will feel more inspired to act than on others. The fluctuation in your energy is normal. Tune in to your physical, mental, and emotional state, your sense of self, and give yourself room for the unfolding process.

Pam's Story Continued

I am a changed person because of this life experience. One truly learns who one's real friends are when a disease like this strikes. Alzheimer's is very scary to some and, to others, a subject you just don't talk about. I am definitely more cynical than the gentle, naïve person I was thirty years ago. But I'm also more generous with my time, and I've learned a lot more things than ever before.

The healing process for me has centered around several things. I have absolutely beautiful new grandchildren. I have loving friends who never left my side, and I've learned that giving is healing.

I do volunteer work with a wonderful non-profit called Share Your Care. They are, among other things, a respite program for families dealing with Alzheimer's or dementia. I'm on their Board of Directors and cannot tell you how rewarding and healing this is for me. It's a pay-it-forward thing that I hope I'm able to do for a long time.

Whatever the experience that has brought you into grief, there is no going forward without some consideration of what that new direction will require of you. Taking time to honestly assess what is needed, what is important, and what is desired will open the pathways in your mind and heart and allow you to make new choices. Trying to rush this process may only exacerbate the challenges. Be willing to sit with your questions and notice the guidance that comes from within you.

For this part of your journey through grief, choose a support resource. What kind of help will support you best at this time? A counselor or grief coach may help you ascertain needs and priorities. A career or financial advisor may help you identify next steps and potential opportunities. Make sure that whoever you choose to consult is fully aware of the circumstances that have brought you to them so that your work together is truly fruitful. Reaching out for this support can help stabilize you while you continue healing.

GENTLE REMINDERS

- No matter how devastated you feel in the backlash of the loss you have experienced, the eternal life force within you is always supporting you and will help you not only survive but find your way again. Trust it.

- Take your time in making all decisions that impact your present and future life. There is no need to push yourself into quick solutions and new identities.

- It can be very helpful to quietly reflect on the crossroads you have come to in your grief. Do not let yourself become frightened of the unknown before you; all will unfold in ways that support your good, if you are willing to just remain open and receptive.

- You do not have to figure everything out by yourself. Engage the wisdom of others who have experienced a similar loss or seek the expertise of qualified professionals.

- Inside your own mind, heart, and soul is the most important guidance on the planet. Take time to reflect, journal, pray, and listen to the voice of the Divine within.

Coaching Yourself to a New Identity

All life changes, especially those that are unexpected or which strike to the heart of your identity, are invitations from your soul. They call to you, asking you to take a risk, to be open, to listen, and to experiment a little with your life.

- **How has your loss affected your sense of identity?** This is a place that needs your loving attention and honest evaluation. Think in terms of your immediate needs in this area. If you have the option, take time making your decisions. Give yourself room to explore possibilities.

- If you must make decisions quickly, as in the case of needing to move or to find employment immediately, **run your choices and options past a trusted advisor.** This will help you gain valuable feedback and an objective viewpoint.

- Remember that every major change can propel you into an extended process of evaluating who you are and who you want to be. New experiences and choices will reveal to you the next steps in your life journey. **Be bold in claiming your evolving identity.** Your soul will support you in these important decisions. Spirit is cheering you on.

SACRED RITUALS
for
Redefining Yourself and Your New Roles

1. Begin a daily practice of prayerful journaling with the specific intention of clarifying your new identity or role in life. You may want to consider starting each writing session with centering prayer, either using a formula or speaking from your heart. The purpose of this prayer is to simply quiet your mind and engage with your God or your Higher Power. The journaling component allows you to put your thoughts on paper and notice new ideas or emerging patterns. Your writing gives you a resource to reflect upon over time.

2. Consider drawing a life map. Identify key milestones in your experiences. Notice themes already present. See how you have survived other challenges and grown as a human being. You may want to reflect upon this map with your counselor, coach, or clergy person. This map may also help you envision new directions. Be sure to look upon your map with soft eyes, with a gentle, non-judging perspective. Boot your inner critic out the door and hold yourself in the grace of compassion and kindness.

CHAPTER FIVE

Reconnecting to Feed Your Soul

"We don't realize it, but when we are going through grief, each day we move toward resolution of our loss. Each day that we grieve, that we deal with painful feelings, is another day that we can add to the passage of our grief."

— Carol Staudacher, *A Time To Grieve: Meditations for Healing After the Death of a Loved One*

Liz's Story

My mother died on July 2, 2007, at the age of eighty. She was diagnosed with an aggressive form of brain cancer in mid-May, and her illness progressed much faster than the doctors predicted.

Everything was so intense during this time. Everything felt dramatic to me. I felt swept up in a fast-moving stream that I did not want to travel down. But I had to hold myself together to try to get out the most accurate information I could for everyone, and in a sense, I had to report the news like a very inexpert Walter Cronkite. Yet I am so grateful that our family, a bit wacky in some ways, was a loving and extremely functional group of people during this time. Everyone brought their very best selves to the situation.

I wanted to spend every minute I could with my mother, as we were very close. However, she had many other family members and friends who also needed to spend time with her, and she had so very little energy to interact with us during much of that time. I am a professional cellist and wanted to cancel my participation in a two-week series of concerts in June, and might have done so if I had realized how brief my mother's struggle would be. In spite of my desire to help as much as possible and to be there for her, it was the music that somehow sustained me in my darkest moments. I felt more grounded because of having to function as best I could in the rehearsals and concerts.

Music was also, in a very real way, the main source of communication I had with her once she entered hospice care for her last ten days. The last thing she asked me to do was to play Camille Saint-Saëns's "The Swan" for her. All she could do was say, "Swah!" since her language was compromised much of the time. We both knew what she meant.

Not every family gets to have this kind of conscious and intimate farewell with their loved one. In this story, it is the loving connection between the mother and daughter that nurtured them both through this difficult passage. Others may have to look deeper – to a comforting memory, to someone else in their family, to a counselor or friend – in order to find nourishment for their soul.

Grief Recovery as an Inside-Out Process

Because grief is such an intensely personal experience, much of the recovery work or healing is done on the inside. What this means is that you give yourself full permission to take all the time needed or desired to be honestly present with your own thoughts and feelings. It is so easy to give in to outer demands and responsibilities and just push ahead without attending to your own needs. If you try to squeeze yourself through the intense and messy emotions of grief and loss, you will be missing an opportunity to grow. Later on, there can be a backlash of unhealed pain.

Our world today does not encourage an inner life, a deep connection to soul and to its essential nurturing. Particularly in times of grief, there are direct and indirect pressures that can distract you from the authentic process of mourning. While there is no such thing as a one-size-fits-all formula for grieving, *all* bereavement work requires some time of sitting with yourself and allowing inner wisdom to wash through you.

Resting in your memories, in the deep places of your mind and heart where treasured experiences are stored, you can find comfort and sustenance that will allow you to go on. These quiet times of inner reflection give you the resilience you will need to eventually move forward. From within, you can draw the strength and courage to face the new landscape of your life. As you honor your inner work, you learn more about yourself and gain a recovery momentum that will invite you to reach outward again.

Essential Self-Nurturing

As your healing momentum grows, it is important to support the new growth by reconnecting with people, places, and experiences that *truly* feed you. Self-nurturing is *essential*; it infuses you with positive energy that will help to carry you forward. At the same time, reaching out and connecting with others can give you much-needed strength.

Self-nurturing can involve any or all of the following practices:

- Daily meditation
- Journaling to release or process emotions
- Maintaining body health through good nutrition
- Exercising to support the body's wellness

- Creating a place of safety, a personal sanctuary, within your home
- Engaging in spiritual practices or rituals that soothe and comfort you

It is easy to fool yourself into believing that you have arrived on the other side of bereavement and that you can now get back to "normal." But you have just passed through a life-changing experience. Healing is a long process; it doesn't happen in a matter of days or weeks or even months. Peaks and valleys are to be expected. And when you reach those wonderful peaks, know that you are healing and be open to all the life energy that infuses you. Hold on to the realization that you are not back at the beginning if you should find yourself in the valley of sadness again.

The Bereavement Cave

Some injured animals crawl into a cave or a hole to lick their wounds. It is their way of staying safe while healing. We humans go into a type of cave by isolating ourselves from others while we grieve. This practice reduces stress and is both necessary and healthy. Yet there comes a day when, in order to embrace life again, we must be willing to leave the cave and seek human companionship.

We are created for relationships. Avoiding contact

with friends, colleagues, family, or others for too long can lead to deeper problems. It is important to help yourself by taking small steps. The actions of getting dressed and getting out of the house can energize your process of re-engagement. Commit at first to short activities, such as meeting someone for coffee or a brief walk. It may feel like even this small step takes an enormous amount of energy, and sometimes it just does.

Liz

After losing my mother, I had everything I needed to have in my life, except my mother. I needed to talk about her a lot. My father and I began walking together frequently. I discovered that we both shared this need to talk about mom often. We cried a lot. We laughed a bit, but I had such an aching sense of loss. I know my dad felt even worse than me.

We all are unique, and each leg of the journey through grief is our own. Returning to usual activities can be an overwhelming energy challenge. However, connecting immediately in familiar settings can also provide comforting structure. Notice what works for you and honor your own needs. Also honor that your needs may very well fluctuate during this time. One day you may feel strong enough to go out into the world, while other days you just want to stay in bed. The days spent in the cave will gradually decrease.

There are no doors on the cave, so you can move in and out with ease.

> If you find yourself soothing your woundedness with alcohol or drugs or other addictive behaviors, please seek immediate help. Those actions only serve to isolate you further, delaying your bereavement significantly. A more dangerous consequence is the potential to develop a lifetime addiction.
>
> Addictions numb the psyche and prevent us from fully engaging in life. While attending to loss and grief is painful, life itself is so valuable and dear that it deserves one's full conscious engagement. If you find yourself in this downward spiral of addiction, invite your Higher Power to infuse you with new courage. Then reach out for help.

Breaking the Seal of Isolation

Until now, much of your grieving may have seemed solitary. There is nothing wrong with that. There comes a time, however, when it is valuable to shift your focus and re-engage with others who can buoy your spirit in fresh or familiar ways. Coming out of the cocoon of woundedness is not always easy. But you have made it this far and you can keep going with the right support beneath and around you.

Sometimes a relationship may appear at first to be supportive simply because it is familiar. Keep in mind that you have changed and your perceptions are different. Your needs have shifted through your loss, and what you expect from others may not match what they think you need. Trust what you feel in response to someone's presence. Consider what would make someone feel safe and supportive to you right now. You can use these observations of healthy interactions with others as your guide:

- The person asks nothing of you and doesn't try to fix you.
- The exchange is more about you than about the other.
- Your silence and your tears are honored just as much as your need to talk.
- Spending time with this person doesn't leave you drained, but gently uplifted.
- The person is flexible and understanding.

Coming out of the cave of isolation will sometimes feel like learning to live and trust all over again. It is a time of creating pathways to a new *normal,* and it may require new friends and a new kind of support group.

Using Your Support Network

When working with clients who are in the bereavement process, Louise often suggests that they take a complete inventory of the people in their support network. This includes listing everyone, both professional and non-professional contacts, that provide some type of care or support.

Consider these suggestions when making your list: *relatives and friends, physician, dentist, massage therapist, coach, mentor, counselor, clergy person, lawyer, financial planner, hairdresser, neighbor, lawn care provider, auto mechanic, home repair contractors.*

Be sure to include phone numbers and email addresses next to each name in your network. Then keep your list at hand, in a convenient, quickly accessible place where you can pick it up at any time of day or night and reach out for the specific kind of help you need. Some people find it comforting to take their list with them when leaving the house. It's like having a friend next to you just in case.

Girlfriends, Mentors, and Coaches

The next steps in this journey require the fuel of caring relationships. You may find that certain friendships provide distinctive healing elements. For example, one girlfriend may be able to see your progress better than you can and remind you that you are okay just as you are. Another may be a delightful distraction on those days when you get too blue. No one person in your support network is going to be able to supply all that you need, yet each one can contribute something.

Women who have experienced a loss similar to yours can be valuable mentors. A mentor is someone who can offer ideas, resources, or insights that may help you understand and accept where you are now. Through sharing her own experience, she offers you a window into *your* healing possibilities. Her experience is her training for this role. A women's group at your church, a grief support group, or even a neighborhood book study group could be sources for connecting with someone ahead of you in the bereavement journey.

Deb's church community was a source of support during and after her husband's open heart surgery. One woman in particular reached out each week to ask about his progress. Because this person was in her eighties and had been a caregiver for her own husband, she carried within her the knowledge, compassion, and ability to see Deb's needs. The important thing was not that Deb spoke at length with this woman, it was that she cared enough to keep asking and, in doing so, held the door of a compassionate listener open. The support of a mentor is sometimes very subtle.

Bereavement and grief coaches are people with great compassion and insight who can also provide support to you as you emerge from grief and re-engage in life. Their training and perspective can offer new resources and strategies for feeding your tender soul. Coaching is not the same as therapy. It is not looking back to analyze the past but to honor your learning in it and integrate the experience so you can move forward. A coach takes you from where you are now in your process to new places of healing.

Here are other ways to tap into the wisdom of women who have gone before you:

- Read about other women who have survived experiences similar to yours. You can find so much at your local library or through doing an Internet search.

- Read books on surviving grief written by wise women, such as those mentioned in the opening quotes of each chapter in this book.

- Look for elders within your own family network and start a conversation with them regarding their losses throughout life.

- Seek out non-familial elder women from your neighborhood or faith community for similar conversations.

• Stay open to receiving the wisdom and comforting embrace of all your sisters in humanity. You never know from what source your soul may call forth just what you need in any moment.

Getting Things On Your Calendar

As you find yourself with more energy, you will want to plan some activities that support your intention to reconnect. Putting things on your calendar adds structure to your days, gives you a sense of purpose and a place of belonging, and re-awakens your joy in living. Another benefit to actually using a planner or calendar is that it helps to organize your thoughts and focuses your energy into the present.

Activities that need your attention will ground you in your life; they prevent you from being swept away in waves of grief or isolating loneliness. As you put something on your schedule, you are making a kind of commitment with yourself – a commitment to stretch a little and to pick up a few more pieces of your life.

Here are some ideas for gently building new structure around soul-feeding activities:

• Find a place to volunteer your time – a place

where your attention is put on others' needs for a little while.

- Say yes to every invitation that comes your way and put them on your calendar, whether you actually go or not.

- Join a book club or other group experience that you think you might enjoy.

- Look for opportunities to attend concerts, lectures, movies, museum exhibits, or other special events that are of interest. Invite a friend to accompany you.

- Take a class in something creative, such as art, quilting, beading, or writing.

- Go on a women's retreat.

- Schedule a massage or some other self-care treat once a month.

Putting things on your calendar validates your life. It says that you have places to go and people who are waiting there to connect with you. It is a visual reminder that life really does go on and that you have a part to play in it.

GENTLE REMINDERS

- The passage of grief is just that – a passage or road that takes you from where you once were to where you are now and to where you eventually want to be. Even when you do not perceive progress, movement is happening at some subtle level. You will move in and out of the "bereavement cave" many times. Each time that you exit the cave of your sorrow and re-engage in your life activities, you are building a path to the new familiar.

- Self-nurturing will be essential during this time. Hopefully you will embrace new habits that become life-long self-care practices.

- Let yourself be surprised by the joyfully spontaneous ways in which the Universe supports your healing. Even if you are still feeling deeply wounded by your loss, challenge yourself to look for and receive the good in life.

- The soul-work of authentic healing requires patience and awareness. Be careful of any tendency to slip into patterns of isolation or addictive behaviors. Take courage in the knowledge that you are growing stronger every day.

Coaching Yourself in Feeding Your Soul

Regardless of what you are mourning, you will move forward much more quickly and effectively by taking the time to nurture yourself all along the way. Self-nurturing practices feed your body, mind, and spirit. It can seem much easier to take care of the body's needs in bereavement than to honor the needs of your inner self, your soul. Here are some suggestions for taking good care of yourself at this sensitive time.

- **Think holistically.** Typically we can get stuck in a pattern of giving attention to only one dimension of our life, such as the physical or the mental. Set an intention that you will put things on your calendar each month that address mind, body, and spirit.

- **Remember to listen to your own thoughts, ideas, inspirations, intuitions.** Your inner knowing will guide you toward good self-care and aid you in choosing the activities most beneficial to you. If you feel the intuitive pull to say no to something, trust that that particular activity is not yet right for you.

- **If you have not already done so, make a complete list of the people and contacts in**

your support network. By making this list you may notice gaps, places where you do not have a trusted contact for a particular area. Use your existing network to find new resources. Ask for recommendations and referrals. Be sure to use this list in attending to your needs.

SACRED RITUALS
for
Feeding the Soul

1. Feed your faith. This is not the time to let go of the faith practices in which you find comfort and solace, but to engage in them more intentionally. Sometimes it can be greatly nurturing to pick up a remembered prayer or devotion from the past. Choose those things that truly offer you the comfort of connection to your own spiritual heritage and to the Love of the Creator.

2. If you have no faith community and regular practice to fall back on, think of what would nurture your spiritual life. Nature, music, art, reading, or a gathering of like-minded people can feed your inner self.

3. Pay attention to the subtle messages that come to you through dreams, images, intuitive nudges, and ideas that seem to arrive out of the blue. Everything in life can inform you and offer direction, insight, and comfort.

CHAPTER SIX

Rekindling Your Interest in Life

"Every loss demands that we choose life again. We need to grieve in order to do this. The pain we have not grieved over will always stand between us and life. When we don't grieve, a part of us becomes caught in the past like Lot's wife who, because she looked back, was turned to a pillar of salt."

— Rachel Naomi Remen, *My Grandfather's Blessings: Stories of Strength, Refuge, and Belonging*

Defying the Gravity of Our Grief

There comes a time in the healing process when it becomes very apparent that, in order to finally close the open wound of our pain, we must be willing to leave the shadows of sorrow and confusion and seek the light of engagement again. This is the time of new choices, and perhaps more choices than we have ever made at one time before. Some choices may turn out to be interim steps that lead to surprising new investments in self.

Even choosing can be bittersweet because choice itself implies what is also *not* chosen. One option must be released so another can be taken.

This moving out of the shadows into the light is a powerful step in reclaiming the life within us that demands to be lived. In a very real way, this movement is the defying of the gravity of grief, the heaviness of deep sorrow. Choice lifts us up. It leads us forward into new possibilities. New choices are the venturing into the future. We must be willing to be led by something greater from within ourselves, something from within our soul that guides and directs us to a waiting opportunity. Moving into the future requires that we pay attention, perhaps pausing often in the quiet to consider who and how we really want to be from this point forward.

Faye's Story

It would be nice to discuss a single loss in detail, but sometimes they come quickly and you must process them simultaneously. I am a swimmer and I returned to the pool after an entire year away, healing a frozen shoulder. My body finally felt strong and the pain was gone; what a blessing. I had missed going below the surface where, in the water, I could hold the noisy world at bay.

We lost my father-in-law, Ken, suddenly in June. He fell down the stairs and hit his head, dying in a pool of his own blood. It is difficult to think of this kind and intelligent ninety-four-year-old man dying in what feels so unjust a manner.

By July some semblance of routine had returned when I unexpectedly lost my job at IBM, where I had worked for twenty-eight years. Nothing had prepared me for all the rejections I received on a regular basis while looking for another job. I find myself looking back over my years as an engineer with awe that I even lasted that long in one company.

I resented the timing of this loss, as my other primary role in life – being a mother to an only child – disappeared with my son's departure for college in Brazil in August. And so we worry about the bills and I go swimming and pull myself through the water and gasp for air, making the pool my hiding place.

Meaning and Motivation

Awakening from grief and loss is like the rising of the Phoenix from the ashes of a fire. You have been through a transformative experience; it has brought you intense pain, opportunities to think of your life in a new way, and a chance to make different choices about how you will live and even about who you will be now. Finding new meaning and motivation for your life is an essential piece in the healing puzzle.

You may have set aside a particular interest,

activity, or pursuit when your life was interrupted or upended by a loss. As you move further away from those initial shock waves and begin to re-engage in life, you will have decisions to make about how you want to spend your days. Like the ripple effect of a stone thrown into water, the waves of grief decrease in energy and intensity and the space between them is lengthened over time. Now you will be able to see more clearly into that open space and choose your next steps.

Only *you* can decide what gives your life meaning and motivation. Think about these simple ideas as you ponder your forward movement:

- Identify interests that have nurtured you in the past and see if there is something you want to reclaim.

- Consider stretching yourself a little by taking a class you have been curious about but never pursued.

- Stimulate your creativity by playing with paint, fabric, words, paper, music, color, or anything you find yourself drawn to.

It may take some time to reconnect with your passion for life after your loss. Your internal clock is always your guide. Be free from the expectations of others that you should behave in a certain way and just return to your "normal" self. You are changed forever. Grief often pulls something entirely new and unexpected from us, and you may now find yourself looking at a completely different horizon.

Facing Your Fears

The uncertainties that arise out of grief can be overwhelming. They can be some of the scariest things you have ever faced. You may discover that you are challenged to look ahead without knowing where the future leads, and you may be called to make life-altering decisions for which you feel yet unprepared. These new decisions may ask you to leave behind the familiar emotional, material, and relational landmarks you have known and relied upon.

As you make the new choices, each one will reveal the next. The very action of facing your fears and taking steps, even if tentative at first, will begin the internal shift toward future possibilities. Facing whatever fear arises is part of the healing process. Trust yourself; trust life. Take your time and know that many steps have no pre-determined schedule. This is another time when self-care will be important. If you push too hard to have the perfect answers, they may elude you, forced out of your vision by too many self-imposed demands.

When facing the inevitable fears of loss and change, it can be very reassuring to talk your decisions through with a trusted professional or friend. Many women also find it very helpful to write everything out in a journal. Putting your thoughts out of your mind and onto paper can give needed perspective.

Be Inspired

Grief is isolating. Coming out of the experience of grief into the daylight of new possibilities takes time and energy. In emerging from the bereavement cave, you put your head up, look out and around, and you begin to think differently about your life. You may discover that you have immediate needs which must be addressed. Staying curious about your options will keep you from going into a tailspin of a desperate pushing to find answers. Be open to inspiration as you begin to move forward.

Stimulate your imagination. Think about what you need and want in the near future. Create a vision board – with words or pictures or both – in which you begin to claim the good needed and desired now. This simple action pulls you out of worry and into a kind of wonder about what might be possible. It gives you concrete images to refer back to when you feel yourself sinking or uncertain. By putting these images on a vision board, you are inviting a response from the Universe and creating an inner space in your consciousness for new good.

Keep this vision board in a place where you will see it every day, yet where it will not be seen by everyone else in the house. You don't need anyone else's evaluation at this point, just your own imagination.

Resurrect old dreams and desires. Loss and its subsequent grief often open the door to the reclaiming of something longed for yet never pursued. Is there a type of work you've been curious about? Take, for instance, the woman Deb met at a class. She shared with Deb that now, in her mid fifties, she is studying in a two-year program to be a medical assistant. She said, "It's something I've always wanted to do and, even though it is expensive, I realized that I needed to go for it and live my dream." This woman is perhaps the oldest one in her classes but is not fazed by this fact. She is focused on her goal of a new career.

Get your body moving. In her book, *Life Changes With the Energy of the Chakras*, Ambika Wauters says:

> *Exercise is vital for managing the tension we accumulate in our daily lives and even more important when we are in the midst of change. It is a legitimate outlet for frustration, pent up rage, and anger. It is a way of keeping the body strong, the emotions stable, and the will engaged.*

Movement is essential to life. It is one of the quickest ways to get yourself out of a depressed mood and back into forward momentum. Set aside a private time to fill your space with music and physically express the new freedom within your heart and mind. Dance away the old and open your arms to welcome new good. Wiggle, chop, kick, roll, bend, sway, swagger, jump, shake, and exhale!

Faye

In Natalie Goldberg's book, Writing Down the Bones, *she says, "Writing gives you a great opportunity to swim through to freedom." And so I now write and think about things like getting my son into the pool before he was a year old. He would laugh while splashing me and stare at all the other babies. He is grown and gone for now; the house is cleaner and more organized, but quiet in a sterile way. Pleasant sounds are missing; my son played all kinds of music and multiple instruments. There were team dinners with lively discussions and energetic dance parties in the basement. I expect and crave the quiet of the pool, but the quiet of the house overwhelms me. A force pushes me out the door to the pool and, my writing circle where I process all the losses. Getting knocked down and then pushing and pulling myself horizontally through the water, a new daily routine is starting to emerge. Eventually, new possibilities will present themselves and I will become vertical and easily move about despite gravity.*

Self-Healing: What is Your Work?

Here are some things to consider as you begin to rekindle your interest in life:

1. *What* really supports you and *who* really offers the kind of support you need? You may find it necessary to let go of old friendships and associations that no longer offer the quality of sustenance you need now. Not everyone will be able to give you what you want; their own experience may not mesh with yours. Be truly honest with yourself about this, because in order to go forward with energy and strength, you will need help and the right encouragement.

2. What nurtures your soul? What kinds of activities fill the cup of your spirit? Take notice of all the things and all the experiences that gently lift you. This could include inspirational reading, meditation, yoga, body work, music, sights and sounds of nature, and physical exercise. Make room in your day or your week to consciously engage with anything that is life-giving.

3. What challenges you? What calls you to move beyond your comfort zone? Thinking outside the box of a previously planned life path can help you find those places where you are now invited to stretch and create something new. Every loss has a potential gain within it. This is a time for self-reflection, to awaken the latent dreams or longings of your life.

Guard Your Own Heart

Even when you are ready to leave the bereavement cave and move ahead with new decisions about your life, it is important to still maintain boundaries around your process. Other people may pressure you to hurry along; they may want the good, old reliable, and familiar you. Others may be uncomfortable watching you grieve; they may even say, "Aren't you over this yet?" But you are changed forever. Something about you will never be the same.

Holding your boundaries at this time is essential. It means *you* decide when, where, and how to re-engage in life; *you* decide the parameters for using your energy. No one else can really know what your loss means to you and how it has impacted you on every level. You can choose to release their evaluations of you. You are not bound by any recovery formula. You may even need to say to someone who wants you to move along faster, "You may be over this loss, but I am not. Please respect my timing."

When you are ready for new or deeper involvements again, you will know it! One day you will realize that it is time to stretch a little and rekindle the fire of your own interests. Remember to be kind to yourself, to breathe consciously and move slowly, to look upon yourself with soft eyes.

The responsibilities and everyday demands of life will always press in upon you, asking for your attention. To have the energy to re-engage in life, you will need to prioritize self-care, not just during this period, but for the rest of your life. This is a time to learn how to lovingly take care of yourself while embracing the road ahead.

GENTLE REMINDERS

- Even while you are healing and moving forward, you will at times look back upon the memories you have of your loss. It isn't necessary to eradicate these memories, only to learn how to hold them without letting them control you.

- Making new choices for your life will lift your spirit and ease the density of residual pain. Be not afraid of choice; embrace it, stay curious about the opportunities before you.

- Be willing to test out new options without judging yourself if some do not work out for you. Remember, something that is not the right fit is still guiding you toward what is next.

Coaching Your Interest in Life

It can take time to figure out how you want to proceed when waking from the heaviness of grief and loss. As your interests in life blossom again, you may want to consider the following:

- **Assess your boundaries.** Check in with yourself to see if you are moving ahead in response to someone else's agenda or from your own inner guidance and desire. You may discover that you don't have good boundaries for functioning in a healthy way in relationships and work. This is a good time to set better limits in order to hold your intentions for self-care. If you have never done boundary work, you may want to look for resources that can help you, including a professional, such as a therapist, counselor, or life coach.

- **Decide to have some fun.** Leaving the drama of loss behind opens the door for inspiration. Think about setting a date with yourself to explore your untapped interests or talents. Is there an activity you enjoyed before that you put on hold during your bereavement? This could be the time to pick it up again and to breathe new life into it. This could also be a wonderful time in your life to try something completely new.

- **To stimulate your interest in life**, you may want to visit an art museum, enroll in a class, attend a concert, or do another activity that is light and undemanding, yet connects you to playful, creative energy.

SACRED RITUALS
for
Rekindling Interest in Life

1. Honor your life and your life journey each morning. Take quality time, even if it is just fifteen minutes, to be still and present in the moment. Feel the beat of your heart; listen to the sound of your holy breath. In this stillness know that you are loved. Take that sense of connection to Source within you out into the day's activities. This will keep you steady and supported in returning to the demands of life.

2. Create a prayer journal or prayer box in which you can leave little notes – a sacred place to express any residual grief, ask for Heavenly help, or just report your thoughts and feelings. By placing these things outside of your body into a receptacle, you free up emotional space for new possibilities. This is a very tangible way to release energy.

CHAPTER SEVEN

Reaching Acceptance

"Life will always be full of challenges and crises. The wise way is not to attempt to find the one path that promises you will never have to endure the pain of loss and illness, but instead to learn how to endure and transcend when unreasonable events come your way."

– Carolyn Myss, *Defy Gravity:*
Healing Beyond the Bounds of Reason

Jennifer's Story

I have lost three children through miscarriage. What came next was a full term stillbirth. The stillbirth is the worst grief I have ever known in my life. After nine months of a normal pregnancy, I had the rug slipped out from under me when at my 42nd week check up I heard the words, "Oh sorry, we don't hear a heartbeat." Sarah Frances was born still at 7:35 a.m. on October 29, 1998. She had ten toes and ten fingers and looked quite peaceful as I held her for what seemed like an eternity, but was really only a few hours.

The most significant thing about my grief was my

experience with the hospital. They took me from a labor room to a recovery room on the maternity floor near the nursery with healthy, crying babies. Because I am a strong person, I made it known that this was not going to work and I needed a different room. They put a sign on my door that said, "Stillbirth." Wasn't it bad enough that I had just gone through fourteen hours of natural childbirth? Now I am known as the woman who had a stillborn daughter.

After arriving home came all the sadness, the blame, the guilt, and the people who wanted to see how we were doing. All I wanted was to be left alone in my world of sadness. How could I ever live to see the next day? How was I going to bury my child?

*As time went on, so did our lives. **The pain never, never goes away.** It will be with me for the rest of my life, and a day doesn't pass that I don't think about Sarah. Three years after my loss, I gave birth to a very special little girl. She is seven today and such a joy. I still hurt for the unknown one…Sarah. How fun it would be to have two living girls who are sisters in every way. I will never be the same person I was ten years ago. I have lost too much, but I am stronger too…in my faith in God and my family and as a parent.*

Changed Forever

The small reminders of your loss can keep appearing for a long time, even for a lifetime. A certain sound, a stranger's profile, a time of year, just about anything can be a trigger that reminds you of the person or situation no longer available to you. These sudden glimpses into the hollowed places in your heart are to be expected from time to time.

Grief recovery is not a drive-through menu of quickly applied remedies. In loss, your sense of security, identity, and confidence can be totally compromised. It takes time to let life reshape itself around a broken heart or shattered dreams. And time alone does not weave the torn tapestry of life back together. The elements of healing need to be consciously and intentionally applied to your pain. Here is a reminder of a few of those elements we consider to be essential to grief recovery:

- Excellent self-care
- Sharing your story with trusted others
- Using your support network
- Attention to the whole self – body, mind, spirit, emotions
- Maintaining healthy boundaries

There is no automatic expiration date on grief! We who grieve do not suddenly awaken one day and say, "There now, I am putting this aside and will never pick up these memories again." Even if we try to do this, there are bound to be memories that sneak in unbidden and threaten our resolve for all pain to be gone. Sometimes we just have to admit, "I am not finished crying about this yet" and let that be okay.

Decide What You Will Keep

Whether your grief was associated with the loss of a loved one, a career, a relationship, a community, or something else important to you, there will come a time for choosing what you will hold on to and what you will set aside. These choices reflect the growing strength of acceptance around your loss. They can be very difficult at times, yet they are necessary steps that bring further healing.

Deb

After my father died, my mother sought my help in cleaning out his closet. She knew that someone else could gain from the clothing she would donate. And while this was her intention all along, she couldn't face the task alone. Somehow my presence gave her the courage to touch my father's things one last time and then let them go.

Together we worked our way through small sections of his belongings. What my mother relished about going through his things was choosing items of meaning to give to other family members. Even in our combined energy we found we could not complete this task all at once. We would bag everything from that day's efforts and then just let it sit in the hall by the door, waiting for energy to move it onward. The thought of letting go of Dad's possessions had to germinate awhile before we could completely release them.

With each item set aside for donation, my role with my mother was changing. Now I was not only her oldest daughter, but a major support person, another adult who could help to manage the home and make decisions. We also went through his yard tools and equipment for maintaining a small farm. Together we realized that Dad's mowing gear was not a good fit for our needs; we needed something smaller and more manageable. We had to give ourselves permission to let go of tools that didn't serve us and replace them with more efficient things. All of this was part of the process of learning to live a new life without him.

It is not just the material things we let go of when we find acceptance and the courage to move on in life. We also decide what memories and experiences we will treasure while reflectively processing others before finding forgiveness and release. Holding on to painful or negative memories will only retard our progress in life. If we give them permission to take up valuable space in heart and mind, they become emotional hooks that drag us back into the muddy waters of doubt and judgment.

Whether it is cleaning out the closet in the hall or the closet in your mind, this process of deciding what to keep is important. Be gentle with yourself. You may choose to keep something now and then realize later that you no longer need or want it. You can travel light; you can be free of emotional and material burdens.

Remembering Wholeness – What to Look For

In the process of reaching acceptance about your loss, it is important to remember that you are a whole being – you are body, mind, spirit, and emotion. Yet unfinished grief will make itself known to you through one or more elements of your human makeup. Here are some things to pay attention to:

• Notice your dreams. Look for any repeating patterns or themes that may indicate you are trying to resolve or work through something in your sleep that you are not addressing during your waking time. You could talk about these repeating dreams with someone or write about them to determine their possible significance.

- Watch out for compulsive decision-making. Keep talking with the trusted people on your support list and ask for advice or counsel whenever you have big decisions to make.

- Be aware of any physical changes in your body. Grief can sometimes uncover physical weaknesses or a medical problem that you were previously unaware of.

- If you have wandered away from a connection to God, this may be the time to seek the comfort and nurturing of a spiritual community. Do not be surprised if you find yourself in a completely different mind-set regarding your relationship with the Divine.

Planting Roots

Grief expands us; it stretches us; it hollows out a part of our inner being and then calls for something new to fill that hollowed part. This may mean planting the roots of new life in some way. It is even possible that everything about you may change, not just your immediate situation but your long-term goals, relationships, and environments.

A new life calls for a bigger commitment of our energy. It asks us to get truly intentional about what we want to be, do, have, and experience from this point forward. On the other side of bereavement is the fertile ground of yet un-named possibilities in which you can nurture new dreams.

These new dimensions of life that are calling you can include: new work or a more satisfying career, adding a room to your home or repurposing an existing space, building relationships or reconnecting with important friends from the past, embracing a new family role or creating new family traditions, engaging in community organizations and activities that feed your soul. The important thing here is not to try to do it all at once or to be instantly successful in all that you try. Let this be a holy process for you. Trust that you are divinely led to whatever will be for your next highest good.

You may find that planting new roots even means opening to a whole new definition of "family." Those you are closest to may not be related to you by blood but by the powerful connection of soulful experiences. You may be drawn into a circle of people who share your grief walk in some significant way. These people understand your loss and celebrate the person you are becoming.

Giving Back

The sense of belonging is essential to a healthy, happy life. Belonging is a two-way street; it requires the give and take of human contact. Many people have undoubtedly helped you reach this point in your grief recovery. In turn, you can help others. Nothing so engages the human spirit as the rewards of extending the hand of help and hope to another.

In seeking a way to give back, to be a contributing member of your community, you will want to consider the unique gifts and talents you can offer for the benefit of others. This does not have to be something grand, just something sincerely given to lift another's heart. It can start with a small step, like volunteering at your church, in a classroom, at a local hospital, animal shelter, or organization whose work and purpose you admire.

In reaching out to help another you will be rewarded, sometimes in amazing and completely unexpected ways. Giving and receiving are equal parts of one complete circle. You cannot give without receiving. It matters not what or how much you give, only that you begin this deeper participation in life. What you have lost can never be reclaimed. But you can gain so much in its place by simply being a vital part of the human community.

When you give to others, you are seeing beyond yourself and the inner focus that grief demanded of you. As you choose to be a larger presence in the lives of others, you are growing and cultivating the rich soil of your future.

Reaching the Other Side and Learning to Dream Again

Reaching acceptance about a great loss in your life is not an easy road, but it is an important road and it offers you the chance to move forward in a whole new way. Acceptance does not negate the value of what you have lost; it honors your memories while encouraging you to reach *beyond* them. Acceptance is a gentle coming-to-terms with your life the way it is now.

During bereavement it may have seemed impossible that you would ever reach a place of peace about your loss. Because your life changed so much, so dramatically, there may have been times when you could not see beyond your present pain and immediate need. Now you have reached the other side, so to speak. You have traveled through the dark night of the soul and have come, once again, into the light of promise.

Through this whole experience of grieving your loss and healing the subsequent woundedness, you have actually always been moving forward in your life, even if you did not feel that growth. In accepting what can never be again, you may find an awakening to a bigger vision of your life.

Acceptance is a sacred passage. You have come out of the cave of your bereavement and welcomed the sunshine of the new self. Never for a moment have you been alone on this journey; your Creator has walked the path with you each and every instant. Now you have new strength to put one foot in front of the other and to dream, hope, envision, and build the framework of your future.

GENTLE REMINDERS

- Be sure that you are attending to your life with loving care and not just falling backward into ambivalence. There is a fine line between compassion toward self and self-pity. You will know you have crossed that line if you are isolating yourself from others in any way.

- Set meaningful and achievable goals for yourself. Consider both short-term and long-term targets you want to reach. Then make a plan for moving toward your goals.

- Continue to seek support that will both encourage you and honor your new growth. Only be around the people who lift you up, who provide unconditional love, and who celebrate the small and large steps you are taking.

- Recognize in yourself the many ways in which you are no longer where you were early in bereavement. Give yourself credit for each step in your healing.

- Be gentle with yourself always and in all ways. Decide that for the rest of your life you will look upon yourself with softer eyes, eyes of love and compassion.

Coaching Yourself to Acceptance

Reminders of your loss will often enter your mind through the years, as in the case of anniversaries, birthdays, and holidays. Rather than resisting those memories, use them as opportunities for further reflection, celebration, and healing. Embrace each memory with compassion toward yourself and the enormous changes you have experienced.

- On a large piece of paper, **draw a road map of your whole healing process**. Mark each milestone with a picture or image, with words, or with small objects that reflect each step of your journey. Use this map to reflect on how far you have come and to encourage yourself to dream further.

- **Go back to something that felt comforting to you** previously in the book and let those words wash over you again and again. Notice how the ideas behind the words make you feel. Highlight these passages so you can quickly find them in the future as you need them.

SACRED RITUALS
for
Reaching Acceptance

1. Grief and loss often bring up opportunities for deep spiritual growth. If you find that there is someone you need to make amends with, someone you want to forgive or ask forgiveness of, do that first in prayer. Then see if there is some action you are called to take to complete another layer of your healing. Forgiveness can be not only a great healer, but also a great equalizer.

2. Whatever your loss has been, it can be profoundly healing to incorporate some ritual activity for letting go. You may find that reaching a new level of acceptance requires you to let go of those things you cannot change. You can do this in prayerful journaling, in your spiritual community, or in sharing your willingness to release the past with someone who truly cares. Let go of unmet expectations, old hurts, resentments, anger, disappointments, and all toxic emotions. They will never serve you.

ACKNOWLEDGEMENTS

"The heart that breaks open can contain the Universe."

– Joanna Macy

We want to thank the courageous women who contributed their personal stories of loss and bereavement to this book. To each of them, **Joyce, Carol, Kellie, Pam, Liz, Faye,** and **Jennifer**, we offer our most sincere and heartfelt gratitude. You are the way-showers in this project; you are women who have reached deeply within yourselves to find the strength to awaken from your grief.

To our readers, we give this reminder – you will not always feel as raw as you do today. You have everything you need within you to rise up and move forward in your life again. Like the force of nature after a forest fire, some seeds of your life have needed the refining heat of grief in order to burst open and reveal new growth.

We believe in you. We pray you the courage to take the next steps in your healing journey. We pray you the enfolding comfort of friends and mentors as you make your way out of the bereavement cave into the light of your future.

We also thank Spirit for the rich and oftentimes awesome guidance that inspired and enlivened our work together throughout this project.

For everything there is a season,
And a time for every purpose under heaven:
A time to be born, and a time to die;
A time to break down, and a time to build;
A time to weep, and a time to laugh;
A time to mourn, and a time to dance;
A time to seek, and a time to lose;
A time to keep, and a time to let go.

– Ecclesiastes 3:1-8

NOTES

NOTES

NOTES

NOTES

NOTES